Jumping the Fence

A Journey from Darkness to Light

KURT CHAVARIE

iUniverse, Inc.
Bloomington

Jumping the Fence
A Journey from Darkness to Light

iUniverse books may be ordered through booksellers or by contacting:

iUniverse
1663 Liberty Drive
Bloomington, IN 47403
www.iuniverse.com
1-800-Authors (1-800-288-4677)

Because of the dynamic nature of the Internet, any web addresses or links contained in this book may have changed since publication and may no longer be valid. The views expressed in this work are solely those of the author and do not necessarily reflect the views of the publisher, and the publisher hereby disclaims any responsibility for them.

Any people depicted in stock imagery provided by Thinkstock are models, and such images are being used for illustrative purposes only.

Certain stock imagery © Thinkstock.

ISBN: 978-1-4620-1267-1 (sc)
ISBN: 978-1-4620-1266-4 (hc)
ISBN: 978-1-4620-1265-7 (e)

Library of Congress Control Number: 2011907144

Printed in the United States of America

iUniverse rev. date: 6/10/2011

Greetings from the Author

Little did I know about the grace of God. He would reveal my lack of understanding and that acquiring the ability to read and write would become necessary to my survival.

Looking back, I wrote the first book Collection By Kurt, a book of poetry because I was told I couldn't. It was only after readers asked me to write another that I decided to write this one, because I could. I once lived in a world without light and love. I discovered that living in the world with them is absolutely wonderful, and nothing should be taken for granted.

To have the opportunity to write about my present life brings great joy. I have found a new life through understanding a few spiritual principles. The wisdom of knowing the difference came by choice, voice, vision, feeling, and manifestation with the acceptance of a free gift. I hope that as you read through these pages, God may bless you as He has blessed me.

Thank you to those who believe and to those I hope come to believe.

Kurt Chavarie
February 14, 2010

Contents

Signs and Wonders

Poetry

Losing My Dreams

First, I want to tell you about the first twenty-seven years of my life. Then, I want to tell you about the next twenty-four years of my life, which have been a dream born out of a nightmare. Let's begin with dreams I had as a child. I wanted to be a policeman, a priest, or even a baseball player.

My preference was to become a baseball player. I enjoyed the Boston Red Sox, and Carl Yastrzemski was my childhood hero. I loved the admiration he received for being a good baseball player. Those who visited our place of residence at the Eastland Hotel and Nightclub often remarked about how good he was as a left fielder and a hitter. When I was of age to play Little League baseball, I was chosen to be on a team called the Angels. My best friend, Mark, was chosen by the Red Sox. I was a little disappointed. I pretended it did not matter, because I was number 3 on the Angels, and everyone said I wore Babe Ruth's number.

I was excited to be on the team, even though I was the smallest Angel. I wanted to run, catch, and hit like all the other boys I watched play baseball. But to me, it was not what I expected. I sat on the bench in the dugout, not playing much baseball at all. Sometimes, the coach let me play when our team needed to get someone on base. Since I was such a small player, the other teams had a hard time pitching to my strike zone. I stood in the batter's box, the helmet down over my eyes, holding a bat I could barely swing. I heard my teammates yell at me not to swing at the ball. Most of the time, I was walked on four pitches and faced more humiliation on my way to first base.

1

The coach told me I was too slow a runner, so I was replaced by a teammate who could run faster. I hated it! I wanted to hit, run, and catch. I wanted to play baseball.

Sometimes during the game, I would roll in the dirt of the dugout to get my uniform dirty. I believed if my dad saw my dirty uniform, he might think I was playing and would come and see me play. I hoped if the coach saw my dad was in the stands, he would let me play. I wanted to be like the other kids, who got to play because their parents were in the stands. I saw the other boys' parents cheer for them while watching the games.

I became an excellent benchwarmer but not much of a baseball player. I was a good Angel, though. I did not hit, catch, or run, but I was good at making my team happy, because the other teams we played could not pitch a strike to me. There were times when the boys on my team would loudly cheer for our coach to let me bat, so we could get a man on base. I enjoyed being cheered for as a Little League baseball player. I received a little recognition and felt worthy of some admiration.

During one game, I received a surprise. I heard the coach call me. "Kurt! You're on deck." I put on the oversized helmet and took a few practice swings with the heavy bat. My surprise came while I stood in the batter's box. I heard the coach say, "Swing at the ball, boy!" I could not believe it! I looked right at the coach, who smiled and motioned for me to swing. "Swing at the ball, Kurt," came from someone in the stands behind me. I turned to see my dad. I was so happy he had come to see me play ball! I had often dreamed of the day he would come. He yelled to me, "Come on, son, hit that ball." I waited for the pitcher to throw the ball. I swung, and with a crack of the bat, I saw the baseball sail over the pitcher's head toward the second baseman. "Look," I yelled to my dad while pointing at the baseball. In my excitement, I did not think to run to first base. I stood there, captured in amazement that I had hit the baseball. I had that moment of joy I often felt when I watched Carl Yastrzemski hit a home run. I felt amazing as I looked at my dad. He was smiling at me and cheering. Everyone was astounded that I had hit the ball, and no one but the coach cared that I had forgotten to run.

I will always remember that ball game with joy, when I had a fan—the only man in my life who mattered to me. He never came to another game, and I never took another swing. In fact, I never played in another game of baseball in Little League. Failing to play baseball as a child crushed my dreams of becoming a baseball player.

My next dream and aspiration came from religion. I often dreamed of growing up to become someone who was admired. I gave strong consideration to becoming a priest. I became an altar boy at the age of seven for St. Peter's Catholic Church in East Millinocket, Maine. I wanted to do a good job, but I was always in trouble for not praying; well, I was not saying my prayers out loud during church services. I remained silent, afraid to make a mistake during the church service. It constantly annoyed the priest that I refused to speak up during the mass. One day, the priest gave me a monthly prayer booklet. He told me to study and recite my prayers, so I could speak out when it was time to say, "Let us pray," during the service. I took the prayer book home, hid it in the garage, and never learned when it was the right time to say a prayer. I was not a good example on the altar as an altar boy. I returned the book to the church, unconcerned with learning to pray on time. It was easier for me not to say a word instead of saying, "Let us pray." As life continued with its own curveballs, fastballs, and changeups, I never "got up to the plate." Just like Little League, I sat and watched life pass without playing as the best benchwarmer I could be and never said a prayer out loud.

The dream I held of becoming a policeman was shot down as well. One day, I needed some money to buy a can of soda for a school activity. I was afraid to ask my mom for some money, but I spotted a quarter on her dresser and took it. After school that day, I came home to an upset mother. After her favorite discipline of a slap to the back of my head while calling me a couple of names, she demanded I go to confession. I visited the church the following Sunday and confessed my crime. However, not only did I admit I stole the one quarter, I added another fifty cents and confessed I had taken seventy-five cents. I did not think I should be punished for just a quarter. I received my penance of saying five Our Fathers and three Hail Marys and was covered to steal my next fifty cents. There was no real justice to become a policeman.

As a child, life outside the home was good. I had friends, and escape with them was easy, as long as the family secret was kept. Things occurred in the house to which a child should not have been exposed. Living above a bar, where town folk came to drink, was not a promising environment in which to be raised. The shame of what went on at our place had left the dream of being a priest back with the altar boy who never said a prayer. Why God would permit things to go on and not answer my cries for help caused me to doubt that God existed.

Mom would get drunk, and Dad would leave. We would end up moving. A promise would always be made that life was going to be different. I did not know the heartache that would be felt after leaving those who had become my friends. This caused me to become indifferent. Why bother making new friends when we were only going to move again? The pain was compounded after every heartbreaking move.

The darkest moments, times, and experiences slowly developed over time. I saw the darkness begin to pervert my mind and fill me with sadness just after leaving Texas and the friendships I had developed there. I had left eighth grade and spent five long days exposed to severe anxiety with Mom and Dad in the car. There was so much anger in my heart that I began to oppress the light with darkness. Self-sufficiency begins while hiding bad motives behind good ones. Survival on instincts became learning life without faith. I needed to hide my emotional stress and run away from the pain seemingly caused by my parents—my father's anger at my mother's drunkenness, her alcoholism, my mother's fear of my father's narcolepsy. Whenever he needed her, she was drunk; whenever she needed him, he was sleeping. Whenever I needed them, I felt a sense of hopelessness and of being trapped with nowhere to turn.

The repeated sounds of fear and anger from them poured into my life, as I sat helpless in the backseat of the car, lost in the darkness of why I was being taken away again from the light and love of my friends. My isolation and desire to build more defenses to the constant offenses permitted me to focus away from what my heart needed, preventing it from getting broken and hurt again. I was heartsick, because I did not understand why this was occurring. I was emotionally unbalanced, because fear and darkness were winning over my soul.

I was unhappy to leave my friends, and it was not safe to express that I missed them. I did not even know it was love I had for them. I only knew it hurt, and I was told it would be better wherever we were going. I did not believe that. I had heard that before, when we left my friends the first time. I was so upset, stuck in the backseat, that I made vows in anger that I would never again believe my parents' promises that life would get better. I pointed blame toward my sister and brother-in-law for allowing them to take me away from their light and love. I became a victim of my own self-pity. Life alone with Mom and Dad, and the difficulties that began to fill my life with guilt and shame, were overwhelming and powerful. The division between my heart and soul began in my mind. I began to fabricate wishful thinking and fantasies to cope when I felt threatened by my parents. This practice of hiding and avoiding them seemed logical when escape was necessary, because confusion and misunderstanding grew deeper, with no reasonable answers as to why I felt such pain. I had no way to release it. I became more indifferent toward light and love, and life itself, as doubts grew into monsters, which made me want to stay out of society. I was abnormally fearful and felt that being an outcast of society was my lot in life. My resolution was to disconnect. For the most part, I experienced only short intervals and glimpses of light and love, and any exposure to these snapshots was destroyed quickly. I let my fears paint a picture from a distorted perspective and clouded by faulty emotions. Most of my perceptions were now created from my mind and emotions, as the perverted darkness called for no contact with any hope my heart might desire. By now, the enemy of my soul had control of my heart with lies so often repeated, they must be truths. "If you were not born, the family would not have these troubles. You're just like your father, bringing unbelievable condemnation." I was slipping into regions beyond human aid, searching for truth within my heart.

I had no faith, I doubted there was a God, I was lost, without conviction there was real love. I doubted true love existed. Un-forgiveness and rage proved to be more suitable barriers to prevent love from breaking my heart. After my parents divorced when I was

5

thirteen, I watched as my father came and went between my mother and his new wife. I have no clue why he did that and am left with bitter disappointment and confusion. I did not understand his remarks about Mom's drinking as the problem; I saw it as her solution. I did not see my mother's alcoholism and drinking as the problem, because she blamed my father for leaving. Her self-pity and misery demanded understanding, so I adopt her attitudes. I, too, felt bad he left. The day he told me he was divorcing my mother because of her drinking led to confusion. After he told me, he and my brother got drunk. He threatened to hurt me, which scared me to death, as I had never seen my father drunk. I denied that her drinking was the reason he was leaving, and soon he appeared with a new woman. He began saying things like, "Do not tell your mother this," and did not want his new wife to know of his visits. He was trying to keep the peace. It was impossible to contain such secrets, and protect him and her, without hurting myself. This added deeply to my insecurity. The unreasonable demands of my father to keep secrets prevented me from understanding what was crushing my heart and my mother's drunkenness made life at home unbearable. The house stank of beer, puke, feces, and urine.

My hunger pangs went unanswered. Starvation and deprivation began to be a way of life, and shame forces me to accept this aspect of life's intolerability. There was nowhere to run. I stayed away as long as possible, walking the streets with anger, fear, frustration, and despair, wondering why I was even born. Life had no value.

My attempts to rest from my weary desperation were denied by the tormented calls of my drunken mother's self-pity. She suffered from her own demons. I prayed to God for a moment of rest, begging, pleading, searching endlessly for reasons why I could not go to sleep or find peace. I was kept awake by my mother's unloving calls and her cries of wanting to die. I was consumed with grief from the loss of rest and lack of food. Relentlessly, she demanded my presence near her, as she lay helpless and hopeless on the couch. I could barely stand being near her, as she was the cause of why the house smelled of urine, puke, feces, and stale beer.

Each morning, I awoke mad at God, because my prayers not to wake up went unanswered. I was full of anxiety, trapped in shame and guilt. I believed that if I were good, she would not be so bad. Every morning, I left home without eating.

Learning to go without food and rest become necessary to my survival of the onslaught of hell I experienced within the realms of my situation with Mom and being in a loveless environment. She drank herself into oblivion every day, always blaming my father. I came home terrified to find her passed out, wondering if she was alive or dead. I approached her carefully and cautiously, watching to see if she was breathing. Sometimes, I was disappointed she was alive. And sometimes, I was relieved she was not dead.

One day, I found a note saying she wanted to die scratched into my bedroom door with a knife. I felt responsible for it all, because had I not been born, this would not be happening. I believed I was doing something wrong, because she cried a lot and constantly told me I was just like my father. I began to hate him, myself, her, and life in general.

My father's desire for me to love him created rebellion, and my mother's demands for attention created rebellion, enough so that I began seeking relief outside the home to cover the full flight from reality in which I lived.

Finding My First Drink

The first time I thought of drinking as something that might be fun was in my junior year of high school. I strongly disliked being alone most of the time during my first two years at Cony High School. I seemed to feel there was going to be another geographic change of life at any time. I was invited by a classmate in my sixth period science class named Alex and his friend John to go to a school dance on a Friday night. The plan was to buy some beer and drink it before going to the dance. I saved my lunch money, and we all pooled what we had and purchased three six-packs of beer. I had no idea what I was in for as I ran into Viles Woods with my six-pack of Michelob that particular Friday night.

I was drinking my fourth beer when I began my denial attitude. Alex said, "Look at Kurt. He's drunk!" I quickly replied, "Oh no, I'm not!" I was having a wonderful time. I was acting stupid with Alex and John before we all went into the school dance after the beer was gone.

At the dance, I met Alice. Alice liked me, and I thought it was because I'd had a few drinks and could make her laugh. The next morning, I did not feel too bad and was excited to think of drinking again. I met with Alex and he told me I had gotten drunk. I maintained that I had not been drunk, because I had not passed out, which I had seen my mother do when she drank too much. I also had not gotten into a fight like what I always heard when my parents were drinking. My father would yell at my mother, "You have had too much to drink!" If no one was fighting, no one had too much too drink. I believed that fighting meant you had too much to drink, and passing out meant you were drunk.

Alcohol was a promising savior that gave me wings to fly, and I could become whatever I wanted after a few drinks. I enjoyed drinking a great deal. It was not long after I began drinking that I was offered the opportunity to buy some pot from a guy who purchased beer for Alex and me. We were really excited this time as we ran up into Viles Woods, because we not only had our beer, but we also had a bag of weed.

Smoking dope, drinking beer, laughing, and joking were all part of the experiences that helped me forget about my life. I found the effects of the alcohol and smoking pot were very desirable. My secret love became drinking beer and smoking pot. My life's purpose was to make plans each weekend that would allow Alex and me to engage in what became our favorite pastime: partying.

I began to cross paths with other students from my school who liked smoking pot and drinking. I often met up with them to get high and drink beer. After a few beers, I thought I had found the answer to life's riddles. I enjoyed the nights I spent escaping into a state of intoxication to forget what life was really like. I came to depend on drinking as a new way of life. Escape via the bottle was a nice solution to a lifetime of emotional difficulty and pain.

Crashing into Destiny

At the age of seventeen, my life fell deeper into the darkness of not knowing the truth about a living and loving God. At that time, I had few experiences that could have been described as evidence of God's love in my life. Each day brought no change from the feelings of emptiness and failure I felt within me. Obtaining courage out of a bottle of booze made my life quite an example of rebellion. There were many attempts and failures to control how I wanted to live my life. But eventually, my suffering became so acute that my only resolution became a wish to die. I turned to drinking with reckless abandon for my relief.

I was heading for self-destruction, and I came close to that one night after drinking myself into oblivion. I was in the backseat of an Oldsmobile convertible, somewhere on a back road in Maine. I was yelling at the driver to go faster and faster. I was strongly tempting the idea of God ending my life. I began cursing the idea of a God who cared about me. I begged for death to come and end my misery of life with an alcoholic mother.

In the darkness of this drunken night, I came to what I thought was the answer to my suffering. I was alone in the backseat of the speeding car, and I wanted to die. Then, from the front seat came a scream of, "Oh my God!" This was followed by the screeching of the tires, as the brakes locked up. The car skidded across the pavement with a flash, as the headlights swept sideways and were shined into the woods. I pressed my face to the car's window to see what was happening. I saw a mailbox on a post coming straight toward the car's window and my face. The car hit the mailbox and flipped over with the sound of crunching metal and breaking glass. My body was pounded endlessly as the car flipped. The car seemed to roll and roll and roll.

The fear was electric as my heart stopped, and my body felt a sharp piercing pain as death arrived for me. I was now out of my body and traveling extremely fast through a long dark and winding tunnel. Two bright blue dots, like eyes, came to be seen in the darkness. I was falling, and suddenly, this incredibly blazing white light appeared before me and drove away the complete darkness. I was being carried into this amazingly warm, wonderful, and brilliantly beautiful light. Time had stopped, and I was in the all-consuming lighted place. I remember looking out over what appeared to be millions of people and seeing a most extraordinarily beautiful place. The people were there watching, as I was laid upon what was called the mercy seat of this being of light. Revelations of my past, present, and future were spoken to me about me. I was told that when it was time to come home, the Lighted Being would come for me. He stood with His hand upon me and said, "Kurt, when it's time for you to come home, I will come get you." There was something I had been created to do upon the earth, and I had not done it.

Before long, I felt like water being poured into a glass as I was returned to my physical form. I began to awaken with a temporal consciousness and was now in the backseat of the car wreck. I saw the driver, Tom, in the middle of the road and yelling words of disbelief that he had smashed his car. The other passenger, Jake, came out of the woods near the car wreck. He was in shock and hugged me after I crawled out the car's window. He was glad to be alive. "We made it! We are alive!" he yelled to me. I remained quite bewildered about what had just occurred.

What was that bright light? What was that light? My disbelief wanted me to deny that I had been taken into whatever that light was. My ignorance said I would be called crazy if I ever told anyone about seeing the light or told of the place. My ignorance said that if that light was God, He did not care about me or I could have stayed with Him. The ignorance convinced me to stay away from that light, because I was being punished. Believing in my ignorance quickly distanced me from the incredible love I had felt while in the light. I remained silent, almost paralyzed, and told no one about the light.

As we waited at the crash site, I began to feel some pain in my lower back. I asked someone who had stopped to take me to the hospital in Augusta. I interpreted the pain as a reminder that the accident was punishment from God, and I went deeper into the fear of not telling what I had really experienced during the car accident. Later, at the hospital, I was informed that my back was broken and two teeth had been knocked out. I kept silent about the experience of going into the light, because I believed it was God's fault I was hurt. I ran away from any light, comfort, or love after that night, October 20, 1979. I remained in a constant state of confusion, certain that the light was to be feared and that hiding in the darkness was good and the only way I could survive.

I was sent home from the hospital and began drinking again. The limitations of having a broken back produced a lot of self-pity. The self-pity only made for many other excuses to begin drinking more frequently. The once weekend-only drinking began to include weeknights. Lots of people visited me while I was confined at home, and a regular place to party was established. My mother's own ignorance and insecurities now became an ally, as she often said, "I'd rather you drank here at home than on some street corner."

When medical confinement to my home ended, I was released to return to school. I found I was no longer interested in attending school for any educational purpose. School became a place to contact other people for information about how to obtain pot and where the weekend party could be found. I began hanging out in Blaine Cemetery, up the street from my house on Winthrop Street in Augusta, Maine, with some other kids from around town. We called ourselves the Outlaws. We were really just a bunch of kids who loved smoking pot. When the responsibilities of attending school got in the way of my desire to smoke pot, I quit attending school. I remained in my own self-created darkness. I began to hang with another gang of kids called the Pirates. We spent the days getting high.

Buying into the Delusion

When I was a very young boy, I was involved in a car accident. I was standing on the front seat of a car, between my mother and her sister, and was thrown through the windshield after we got hit head-on by a drunk driver. I still have the scar on my chin. As a result of that accident, a trust fund was established in my name. When I reached my eighteenth birthday, I was permitted access to that trust fund of five thousand dollars. Getting my trust fund money allowed me to dig deeper into the darkness, while evading most of life's responsibilities.

I spent half of the trust fund money to purchase my first car. It was a silver and burgundy AMC Hornet. I kicked the tires and turned on the radio before telling the salesman I wanted the car. The car helped me believe I had freedoms and privileges now that I had reached the age of eighteen.

I did not want a job; after all, I had the rest of the trust fund money to do with as I wanted. I had another lawsuit pointed at the driver from when I injured my back. It was nearing the time for settlement on that insurance claim. So, I did not see any real need to get a job. I had the delusion that, as an eighteen-year-old with all this money, I was a big shot.

Everyday drinking and twisted thinking caused by smoking dope finally brought the need to escape to another place. I had a desperate feeling that something in my life needed to change. The kind of happiness I first found in a bottle of booze lessened while living in Augusta, Maine. I believed moving to another place might bring the happiness that had disappeared while living in Augusta. My mother had moved to Rockville, Maryland, to live with my sister. I considered following her.

The insurance settlement was reached, and I received another fifteen thousand dollars. My new car and graduation from high school offered me the opportunity to leave town. The money gave me the freedom to run away from my problems. I arrived in Rockville, Maryland, on the doorstep of my sister and her husband. Though they were glad to have me, I was suspicious. I believed it was only because of the money I had. I agreed to pay them a very small amount to live at their home. I began sharing a space with my mother in the basement in their home. It was not what I had expected to find. Living in the basement brought a lot more disappointment and discouragement. What was I going to do with my life now that I was not in school? I felt pressure to be successful. A career was most important and more imperative than ever, and I had no idea what to do with my life.

Living near Washington DC, and the possibility of a lifestyle that included drinking at bars was a nice invitation of where to consider finding my career. I was like a fish out of water and began to clamor for some emotional security. Strange as it may seem, a nearby barroom called the Bitter Lemon Pub became my sanctuary. It reminded me so much of the barroom I grew up in back in East Millinocket, Maine. I spent my nights sitting on a barstool, drinking beer, and hoping to find a girlfriend. Each draft beer that passed my lips reduced the awkwardness that came with being a punk with a lot of money in my pocket. Finding a girlfriend represented a certain measure of success for me. One more beer was always necessary to give me the confidence to go talk to some of the barroom girls. But, I never actually seemed to move from my seat to speak to these girls. Instead, I was consumed with my drinking and need for courage to go meet these girls.

My family wanted me to get a job, but I didn't really understand why I should get a job when I had all that money in the bank. If getting a job was just to make money, I was not really in need of getting one at the time. But, I finally decided to accept my mother's suggestion to find work as a bartender. My sister was pressuring my mother to make me be responsible, so Mom suggested I attend a bartending school. She sold me on the idea of becoming a bartender when she suggested that I might meet a girl and make new friends there.

I attended the International Institute of Bartending. The school was exciting, and I learned the chemistry of mixing alcohol with sodas or fruit juices to create mixed drinks. I heard names like martini, Tom Collins, Bloody Mary, and screwdriver at the school. They were names I had heard as a child growing up at the Eastland Hotel, the hotel and nightclub my parents had owned in East Millinocket, Maine. I enjoyed making small talk with my mother. She had tended bar for years and knew about the drinks I was learning to make.

Discovering Work

I graduated from the International Institute of Bartending and was given a long list of potential places for employment. It was interesting to learn of the many different kinds of establishments that had barrooms. Some had live bands; others had a jukebox. Some maintained a dress code. All offered me a different atmosphere for a variety of entertainment. Country bars, rock-'n-roll places, jazz clubs, and strip joints were all on my list. My favorite place to look for a job was a barroom with a jukebox. I traveled around Maryland, Virginia, and Washington DC, seeking work, but I was never interested enough to get on the other side of the bar. The music, the lights, and the women all contributed to a constant chase after this illusion of where I thought I could find happiness.

The Bitter Lemon, which served only beer and wine, was just down the street from my sister's home. They were looking for a bartender, so I decided to apply. I sat at the bar drinking, trying to muster the courage to ask the guy next to me, Bret, what he thought of the place. After a few drinks, Bret told me he liked to have a beer or two before going home, and the Bitter Lemon was just around the corner from his place of business. Bret was the co-owner of a swimming pool company. Our conversation led me to admit I was looking for a job, and after buying several beers for each other, Bret asked me if I wanted to come to work for him.

The next day, I was at the swimming pool company office, just a block away from home, with a new job. I did not care what I had to do.

It was a money-making opportunity, and I could now tell my mother, brother-in-law, and sister that I had a job. I came to and left from their home as I pleased, and I often did not see them for days. My late-night drinking and early-morning hangovers caused me to avoid spending time with them. My drinking at the Bitter Lemon Pub and the Silver Fox Tavern became my way of life every night after work. I enjoyed drinking all night, dancing sometimes, and occasionally meeting a woman with whom to have a drink.

Looking for Love

Once in a while, I would go down to M Street in the Georgetown part of Washington DC, to drink. On a few special occasions, I would find a woman on Fourteenth Street before attending the bars. I was looking for the companionship and love that was guaranteed by spending my money in the right way. I did not like buying drinks all night for a woman and never seeing her again. The women on the streets taught me about love through sex. I didn't know anything about my desires for a woman. I was never given the father and son facts-of-life talk. The mystery of the birds and the bees was discovered on the streets by ladies of the night. I once found a pile of *Playboy* and *Penthouse* magazines and thought I was getting educated. Most of the time, I really felt alone, and most of the women I met were companions for only a night. Sometimes I got a date, but nothing consistent ever developed—except the belief that's just how it was.

Finding a love life couldn't interfere with the love of drinking, which never left me alone. I always felt like a drink. One night, I met Kelly, a beautiful young girl with green eyes and blond hair, at the Silver Fox Tavern. While listening to her story, I became convinced that I could rescue her. I felt sorry for Kelly that night, and my life's mission suddenly became to save her. Talking about the money I had, along with her dancing, sweet figure, gave way to what would become my second devastating accident.

Falling in Lust

Kelly and I began spending all our time together. Drinking and dancing were our nightly routine before bigger troubles began for me. One night a driving-while-intoxicated arrest changed our way of life. We needed a new plan after I told a lie about cleaning a pool that I did not clean that ended my employment with the pool company. I had, by then, spent all the insurance money and was broke and jobless. But, I was still deeply in lust with Kelly. I called my dad back in Maine for help. When I was in trouble, it was my habit to call him. He suggested moving back to Maine and told me he knew of a potential job. I could get a Maine driver's license and a new job if I moved. I called Kelly, and we decided to leave together. We took off for Maine late one night. The situation created a lot of fear, and Kelly began to show much more disapproval of my drinking. I vowed to her I would not drink so much.

Kelly and I arrived in Maine, and the solution to my drinking became a job working nights at Pine State Tobacco and Candy Company. I no longer had the time to stay out on weeknights like I had back in Maryland. I had a new lease on life, a new attitude all around to behave, a girlfriend, and a new job. If only it had been that way just after high school, I would never have had to leave to find such success in life.

We got ourselves a nice apartment. Kelly got a job at Bonanza, and we thought we had it made. We were engaged to be married, and work was going well. We both had jobs, the bills were getting paid, and we both felt that getting married was the next best thing

19

to do. In celebration of our successful lifestyle, we began going to bars on weekends. Our nights out on the town drinking and dancing soon disintegrated into severe arguments. After several drinks, we would begin bickering about money or other people's attention to us that brought out our insecurities. We would make up during the week while separated by our jobs. The weekends brought bitter discontentment, until I decided to just give up. I got stinking drunk one day while Kelly was at work. She was so upset that I had gotten drunk without her. During our fight, I told her to leave. Kelly called her parents to come get her, and she returned to Maryland.

I stayed in the apartment and kept my job at the warehouse. I continued going to work every night, but my job now seemed to demand too much and pay too little. I questioned the reason for this sudden hardship. Another drunk-driving charge on one of my weekend celebrations without Kelly only added to my problems. Self-pity covered the fact that I really missed her, my first love, and that I regretted telling her to leave.

The Descent

Reaching the age of twenty was most difficult. Without Kelly in my life, I began having severe episodes of anxiety and depression. I gave up my job and my apartment and went back to Maryland with another resolution. I wanted to get back together with Kelly and I was going to quit drinking for good. I thought I had found a firm resolution and answer by returning to Maryland. I got my old job back with Bret at the swimming pool company and found a place to live. Yet, something was very different. I grew desperate and frustrated by wanting to spend time with Kelly. She now had her own place and the needs and responsibilities that meant. I began to sneak drinks on the nights we were not together on a date. It was not long before this caused her to give me an ultimatum to quit drinking or stay away. "You're the weakest man I know," she yelled after catching me drunk once after work. I was forced to choose, and the nights I stayed away from her, I got drunk. The time I spent with her, I stayed miserably sober. I hated this way of living.

Then, I got a call I thought was my saving grace. Kelly called with the news she was pregnant. I was absolutely delighted. I told her I would marry her and quit drinking. She said she would think about it. A few days passed before she called me to give me the answer to my proposal. I was devastated when she rejected the idea of getting married. I begged her to reconsider, but to no avail. I told her I would quit drinking. Kelly called me again a week later and told me she was going to have an abortion. This was devastating news. I tried to understand why she would consider doing such a thing.

21

Her decision began my descent into the bitter morass of the deepest self-pity. The darkness overwhelmed me, and I needed a way out. I needed a drink!

I ran to the Silver Fox to drown my sorrows. I sat on the barstool, trying to think of a way out of the terrible mess in which I found myself. The pain of my life was overwhelming. I thought her pregnancy was proof that love existed between us. *How can she do this? How can I stop her?* These questions plagued me. Her desire for an abortion seemed to deny our love's existence.

I was drinking with purpose, searching for understanding. I looked to the guy sitting beside me at the bar for understanding. I wanted to take a long trip and never come back. I wanted to die. My newfound providence was in his smile, a handout, and a voice that said, "Take two, that's plenty." I took five of the several hits of LSD this other soul held in his hand. I got up and walked away from my barstool providence. I was convinced I was doing the right thing.

Killing of Myself

I was alone in the darkness and ignorant in my belief that abortion was actually murder. The loss of my belief in love put me in complete emptiness. With no further reason to go on living, I put all five hits of LSD in my mouth at once. I never wanted to return to the reality of my pointless life. Time came and went, the music stopped, and the people left. I had blacked out from consuming so much alcohol and high-powered chemicals. I ended up lying in a field behind the bar. I struggled to get off the ground, but I felt chained to the earth. The earth was slowly swallowing my chains, pulling me closer to what would become my death site. Like quicksand, the earth seemed to be trying to wrap itself around my body and pull me down into death.

I was fighting for my life while I tossed and turned, struggling to get away before I was swallowed into the earth. The tall grass thrashed like whips on my hands and prevented me from removing the chains on death's door. The trees above me said it was wrong to have taken my own life. Images of life forms in faded shadows were yelling and screaming around me. The violent struggle between life and death continued, and I heard, "No, no, no," over my attempts to get away. A giant grasshopper stood before me. He was weeping and gnashing his teeth while announcing he was king, and his army would soon arrive to devour my flesh and leave only my soul. Other voices grew louder with tormenting laughter, as the giant grasshopper's army marched closer. His eyes were lifeless, a soulless brown, glaring at me like I was a feast for his army.

The shadows grew thicker; the shouting trees became louder.

This sent shivers throughout my entire body. "Why did you take your life?" was repeated over and over. I felt the cold hand of death approach me, when I finally broke loose, got up on my feet, and ran. I stumbled out of the field onto a pathway. Stopping to look in which direction to go, I was startled by another voice. Breathing heavily, with my heart pounding, I turned around to find a huge, ugly, black demonic figure. His voice boomed at me, "Where do you think you are going?" He was blocking what appeared to be my only way out.

I said, "I need to get out of here. I made a mistake!"

The demon laughed and in a malevolent voice said, "There is no way out of here!"

I said, "I need to leave. I need to find God!"

The demon growled in anger again. "God is not down here!"

Again I said, "I need to find God and tell him I made a mistake!"

The demon yelled back at me, "You should not have taken your own life!"

I said, "I need to go. I did not know I would come to this place."

In the lighter shadows behind the demon, a short distance away, there appeared another image, more human in form. The demon stepped aside and said, "Go!" I ran past the demon and toward the other being. I got closer and saw that it was not a human being but appeared to be the image of one. It was the devil Satan himself, and he was laughing at me!

Grinning, he said, "Your soul is mine!"

I denounced him. "God is going to be mad at you for tricking me."

He shrunk back in terror and then leaped at me with pathetic confidence, saying, "God is not here! God does not want you! God left you! I tricked you all this time. Your girlfriend lied to you also. God does not love you, and you never loved her, or you would not be here."

I argued back, "Oh yes, I do," and demanded—and then begged—that he leave her alone. It was not her fault but mine, and I pleaded for him to leave her alone. I was now in the deep murky shadows, lost within this kingdom of darkness. I felt totally disconnected from the life I had had before I arrived at this place. I was far worse off than I was before I left the bar.

Making My Deal with Satan

I was unaware of how this crafty devil captured souls, and I made another mistake: I promised him I would never love again. He just smiled at me. "Your soul is mine. It's in a box now. Come with me." I could do nothing but follow him into the blackness of the darkest night of my life. I continued crying out that I had made a mistake but to no avail.

The things that occurred in the blackness of this place were unspeakable abominations. I felt lost between what was real and unreal. I awoke in the bedroom of my apartment. My clothes were all torn and dirty. I could not trust anyone or anything now. I felt forsaken and lost, and there was no one to call. I had very little money. I decided to quit my job that day and gathered up a few things to sell. I left the house, pawned the items for a bit of money, and went to get drunk yet again. I wanted to forget it all. I knew I was in trouble, and I prayed and prayed all the time, but to no avail. I truly was lost, frightened, and purposeless. My fate seemed sealed in this endless desperation and unending thirst for a drink and a smoke every day, all day! I could not get or stay drunk enough to blot out my relentless fear. I passed into regions far beyond human aid and understanding.

The guilt of my passions for Kelly and the remorse over my drinking drove me deeper into seclusion, and I ran from the city of Rockville, Maryland, back to the woods of central Maine to hide. I got my job back, working nights at Pine State, and I spent each and every day outside of work at my apartment in the oblivion of drunkenness. I became a reckless recluse and a total failure at life. I felt the gates of hell clang behind me after receiving a Christmas gift from a co-worker. She gave me a fifth of vodka, and I went home that night and began drinking the spirits in that bottle. It was the night before Christmas Eve, and I was alone in my apartment, enjoying the gift. The people above my apartment were having a party. I turned on my stereo to drown out the noise of their party. I was drinking and listening to Black Sabbath and began to think about Kelly and the awful injustice of her having an abortion. The more I dwelled on my past, the more I drank, and the more I drank, the louder the music got. The louder the music got, the more the people upstairs banged on their floor, perhaps wanting me to turn the music down.

The last thing I remember is answering the door and finding the police. I came to in a jail cell. I was let out on my own personal recognizance. I found a court summons in my pocket for disorderly conduct. It was Christmas Eve day, and I walked home very early in the morning. I found the empty bottle of vodka in the driveway of my apartment building and became upset, wondering who had drank it all. And, who gets a disorderly conduct charge while alone in their apartment?

My friend Jake, who was in the car with me the night of my car accident, came to visit me. We went out drinking, like we had done so many other times. Jake and I went to the town of Gardiner, Maine, to a place called Margaritas. We both left fairly intoxicated.

Jake was driving when we ran a red light and were hit by another vehicle. Jake continued driving, and I blacked out. When I came to in my apartment the next morning, I had a court summons for criminal trespass in my pants pocket. I called Jake, and his story was that I passed out in some lady's yard. He said we had a blowout caused by the crushed fender, received in the accident, rubbing against the tire. I could not remember and went to see a lawyer about the criminal trespass charges. I told the lawyer about passing out in some lady's yard. I asked if he could tell her I was sorry and maybe ask her not to press charges. The lawyer told me to meet him in court the day I was summoned to be there.

I got a haircut, put on a suit, and went to court at the appointed time. I sat in court, waiting until the lawyer came to me and said, "Kurt, you're going to have to plead guilty to this charge of criminal trespass."

I said, "I am not guilty. I got a haircut and put on this suit for court today to see the lady."

The lawyer looked at me strangely and said, "You're not here to see the lady. You're here to see the judge, and he is blind. Kurt, you were found in the police department. They escorted you outside and asked you not to return. They told you if you returned to the station, they would arrest you, and you defiantly and belligerently returned, cursing. You will plead guilty to this and pay a fine."

The events surrounding that encounter with the legal system scared me. I had been absolutely clueless about what had happened, and I didn't like the control alcohol was exerting over me. I made countless attempts to stop drinking over the following years, and they all failed. I lived in a spiritual hell caused by my mental obsession for alcohol and the physical cravings that continued keeping me in a soul sickness. I stayed in this vicious cycle until I met another opportunity for better understanding. I received another drunk-driving charge.

After work one day, I defiantly got drunk. I was relieving myself behind a store and cursing at people who looked at me as they passed. Their complaints reached the police department, and the police found me before I could get out of town. I failed the field sobriety test.

A Prisoner of Contempt

The embarrassment of my fourth drunk-driving charge. The confusion of trying to live by the rules. I was pretending to be good while doing things that were wrong and had me heading for judgment day. I was faced with the certainty that the end of my freedom and right to live in drunkenness was coming. It was in a courtroom where I first heard a prayer for me, as the judge said, "Mr. Chavarie, it appears you have a drinking problem. May God help you." Until that day, knowing any of God's love had never seemed possible or absolutely necessary. This day of judgment over my behavior came with clear evidence that I was a hopeless drunk and that I needed the help of God. The judge sentenced me to get help for my drinking problem as well as six months in jail, with all but thirty days suspended. I was court-ordered to seek alcohol counseling and put on supervised probation for two years. I had to pay a fine of five hundred dollars, and I lost my privilege to drive for two more years. At the tender age of twenty-five, my world was ending, and I was going to jail.

My vivid imagination terrified me about what to expect in the county correctional facility. Visions and voices from television shows I had watched provided the basis for a terrifying perspective of what it would be like. I was relieved to find that there was nothing sexual, which I had feared would happen. But, it was humiliating to wear a uniform with the word "PRISONER" stamped on it.

Armed guards directed everything that went on inside: when to wake up, when to eat, when to shower, when to play, and when to work. There was a complete loss of liberty, and I had nothing but time to think about the loss of the privileges I had taken for granted.

While at the jailhouse, I met a man named Bill. He was there, with three others, in my cellblock. Bill was from Boston, a city boy who was in for fraud. He and I collaborated to hoard cigarettes and candy with our weekly spending money. We would then bribe other prisoners to do our work in exchange for the candy and cigarettes. They made our beds, washed the cell floors, and changed the channel during the few hours we got to watch television. This made us the "big shots" of the cellblock. One visiting day, Bill's girlfriend smuggled in a joint. We smoked the pot. I got so stoned and paranoid I became convinced I was going to quit when I got out of jail.

I flirted with disaster after my release from jail. I did sign a contract not to drink any alcohol for a year. I quit for nine months and then began drinking again. I drank until the suspension of my driver's license was fulfilled.

I needed to get my driver's license back, and I became concerned about my drinking. I went to visit an alcohol counselor at New Directions, in Augusta. The counselor referred me to Turning Point, an alcohol rehabilitation center. I was screened for a drinking problem. I failed the screening test, which indicated that I was a chronic alcoholic and was referred to a treatment plan for alcoholism.

Last Call

A twenty-eight-day outpatient program through Turning Point Alcohol Rehabilitation Center was mandatory. After completion, I might get back the privilege to drive a motor vehicle. To attend the center's programs, I needed a concerned person to consent to my enrolling in the treatment, so I called my father. I had to convince him I was finally going to stop drinking before he agreed to be listed as my "concerned person." I was put on a list to enter Turning Point and be treated for alcoholism.

I had a two-month waiting period before entering rehab. It gave me time to obtain a better personal understanding of alcoholism. I remained sober for thirty days before I tried the drinking game again. I saved a thousand dollars by not drinking between June and July of 1987. I decided to take a vacation to Maryland. While on the plane, I ordered a beer. I thought no one would know if I had a drink. The guilt after the first sip was so extreme that I had to order a second beer to cover the remorse I began to feel.

I was confused, and I begged and pleaded with myself to understand the good in quitting drinking. I had to drown the feelings of guilt and remorse, so I spent the next ten days drinking around the clock at a beach in Ocean City, Maryland. I'd rather drink and die than concede that I might be an alcoholic and have alcoholism. I was so ashamed that I could not drink safely. I really was a weakling, as Kelly had said.

Things I experienced during those ten days convinced me that I had a real drinking problem: a car accident, a fight, being with a married woman, passing out in public, feeling like crap every morning. These were all signs I had no control of what might occur after I began to drink. I also realized that the one man who had chased me all my life to stop drinking was, in fact, right about how it would ruin my life—my father, to whom I had lied so many times about drinking. My father, who had bailed me out of so many jams when I needed money. My father, who had risked being yelled at every time he mentioned I should stop drinking.

I thought of him and called him before my return to Maine. He was excited to hear from me, and I asked him to pick me up at the Portland Airport. He was under the impression that I had not been drinking, since he had agreed to be the concerned person for my attendance at Turning Point. I hung up the phone and decided to get drunk: the binge to end all binges. I was terrified of what life would be like if I quit drinking. I was also terrified as to what might happen if I continued drinking. I reached complete defeat after ten days of hard drinking. I was willing to surrender to the idea that maybe I had a drinking problem. I still insisted that it was not my fault that I drank. My last night of vacation, I still drank.

I awoke after drinking to oblivion. I was in a friend's truck in a field in Ocean City, Maryland. I smelled like a brewery that had been burned down by cigarettes. My hair and clothing were in shambles as we took off for the Baltimore airport. I was so hungover and beaten down, I actually looked forward to attending the alcohol clinic when I got back to Maine. I was so defeated, as I slowly made my way through the airport to my departure gate. I had a layover in Pittsburgh, Pennsylvania, before traveling on to Portland, Maine.

I walked slowly through the airport in Pittsburgh. I looked so bad and smelled so awful that people were going out of their way to avoid me. I found a barroom and thought a drink would help. I went in and stood at the bar, waiting to order my drink. The bartender was a pretty blond woman. I soon became upset that she was busy and did not notice me, standing there at the end of the bar. I barked at her that I wanted a 7 and 7.

As I waited for her to make my drink, I became anxious in anticipation of getting that drink into me. The idea of what it could do for me made me quite impatient. I took the money out of my pocket; I had just enough for two drinks. My hands shaking, I placed the money on the bar. The bartender returned with my drink, and I nodded for her to take the amount I owed out of the money on the bar.

I was so ashamed and did not want her to notice that my hands were shaking. Not only were my hands shaking, my body was quivering and shuddering for some relief. The bartender turned her back and walked away with the money. I grabbed the drink with both hands and brought it to my mouth. I swallowed the entire drink before returning the glass to the bar. Oh yes! I sighed, as everything now was so nice. I considered marrying the bartender for bringing me such comfort.

Complete Defeat

The plane arrived in Portland. I got off and walked through the airport, searching for my father. He was standing with a big smile on his face. His eyes were beaming brightly. He was a tall man, full of pride and happiness to be there for me. We met with a handshake, and his first words to me put me in the darkness, as I met with the four horsemen of fear, terror, bewilderment, and despair. Smiling, he said to me, "So, son, how long has it been now since your last drink?" My head dropped, and my mind raced for the right answer. Rage that he would dare ask such a question hit me. Confusion followed, as I searched for an explanation and to get some satisfaction out of the right answer.

Terrified and angry, I looked up into his shiny eyes. I was ready for another fight about my drinking. I said, "Well, Dad, I took two drinks back in Pittsburgh." That was all I was going to reveal. I watched his eyes fade to a lifeless gray and his head bow.

He shook his head and mumbled, "You're killing me, son, killing me." He turned his back and began to walk away. I wanted to yell, *Stop, you do not understand, I needed to drink! Wait, I promise I will never do it again! Dad I am sorry, it's not my fault.* These were the unvoiced screams, as the hole inside me opened and began to swallow me. I wanted to yell that it was his fault for leaving me to a drunken mother as a child. I wanted to tell him Mom said I could drink. I clamored for something to stop the feeling that came when he turned his back on me. I was completely lost in a terrifying loneliness that no hope could enter. I followed him to the car. Driving home the next

33

hour was full of a kind of silence I never want to experience again. He dropped me off at my apartment, and I made another resolution that I was going to stop drinking.

It was in the rehabilitation center that I began to think it might be possible to stop drinking. It relieved me to know that I was sick, not crazy. The treatment program revealed to me that I was dying of chronic alcoholism and drug addiction at the age of twenty-seven.

One night at the rehab, something happened that made me almost quit attending. The instructors made us sit in a circle. One by one, we went around the circle, and each person had to say something nice about himself or herself. When it was my turn, I blurted out that there was nothing good about me. They seemed harsh and cruel when they did not agree. An instructor said, "Go home and think of something; we will ask you again tomorrow night." I did not sleep all night, as I tried to think of an answer to the question.

I almost did not return to the rehab the next night, but I decided to fight with them. I sat in the circle with the others as they asked the same question. When it was my turn, I said, "There is nothing good about me." No one replied, and it felt like I had a sword stuck in my heart. I bent over in my chair and shouted, "I've got a nice smile, so I have been told, but I don't believe it."

Everyone in the room clapped, some laughed, and someone said, "Yes, Kurt, you have a wonderful smile."

Seeing the Light

I began to understand some of the tragedies of alcoholism. I still believed that it was not my alcoholism but what I had experienced growing up in a barroom that was familiar in the stories I heard. I was not that bad and too young were common rationalizations I used to distance me from the others in the group. They called this denial, which meant I did not know I did not know. I was introduced to a set of principles they described as a design for living. After twenty-eight days, I graduated from the program at the rehabilitation center. I had completed everything in order for me to have no more legal problems.

As I waited for my driver's license, I remained sober for ninety more days. I still rebelled at times about asking for help. My soul was dying, and a fence of insurmountable loneliness surrounded me. I could not jump this fence until an indisputable miracle of hope came into my life.

It was a Friday night, when I came to believe that a living, loving God truly existed. I spent a lot of time alone, isolated and trying to figure out what to do. How was I to live with the knowledge that to drink was to die? I knew that would not keep me from drinking. I was like a ping-pong ball, bouncing back and forth between wanting a drink and not wanting one. I remembered that a rehab counselor had suggested I ask God for help. I was at home upset at what I had been told.

That night, as I lay in my bed, I felt awkward to be at home on a Friday night. In all the years since I was seventeen, my Fridays were spent somewhere getting drunk. I needed God's help, as I had no clue what to do with myself. I wondered how was I going to go dancing, go fishing, do anything now that I could not drink. I considered asking God for help, but I had no idea how to pray. It felt extremely unnatural that I was home on a Friday night. I knew my life was miserable without a drink. I also knew I was miserable, because I had drunk too much. At that moment, I could not see life with a drink or without one. My mind continued racing and debating whether to go out to drink or ask for help.

Crying Out

That same night, I paced back and forth, wondering what to do. I wanted to stop the awful experience of bargaining, and for several minutes, it seemed endless. I would pick up the phone, wanting to ask the counselor for help. I would place the receiver back down and curse that no one would understand. I went to the door, wanting to leave for a drink, and then stop and return to my room. I became more fearful and angry. This went on for a while. Then, I heard one peculiar, faint, soft voice. It came in a whisper and kept saying, "Ask God for help! Ask God for help! Ask God for help!"

I rebelled against the idea until I felt like I had been kicked in the back of the legs and brought down to my knees. I heard a louder and more direct commanding voice say, "Ask for God's help to do something for you."

Several times I cried out, "God help me! God help me!" After each yell, I sensed a warm feeling come into the room and surround my body. I got back up on my feet as this warm feeling passed through my body. I stood in awe, feeling a sense of calm like none I had ever felt. It was then that I could see drinking was not the real answer. Now, my mind was at such peace, and my body was so relaxed. I lay down upon my bed, wondering how long it would last. I fell asleep and slept like a baby.

On awakening the next morning, I realized that I had just experienced my first night of real sleep. I had not worried myself to sleep or drank to pass out, as I had always done before. I had not woken up to face the darkness alone. It was clearly obvious that God had removed my obsession and compulsion for alcohol. I felt so wonderful I thought something must be wrong with me. I believed this was a second chance granted by God and perhaps my last chance to stay alive. I came to believe in God and to pray to Him. I had a thirst for more knowledge of His will.

Believe It or Not

It was after God's grace removed my obsession for alcohol that the new desire to love began. I began to attend church, and I was baptized in the name of Jesus. I began taking altar calls and, once, specifically asked for help to quit smoking. The pastor came over to me, laid his hand on my head, and prayed in Jesus's name that the spirit of nicotine be cast out. I felt it was and did not smoke for a week. My job at Pine State was working in the returns and damages department. It was a place full of tobacco products. I doubted the idea that it was a spirit that was cast out and decided to smoke after a week. I missed smoking. Besides, it was not giving me the trouble drinking did.

I made several visits to the church before I began to feel empty again. I quit attending that church. A short time passed before my former pastor came to see me at my house. He came in and began telling me I was full of the devil. He said it was his job to look after his flock. I began to pray to God for protection and truth. I was unsure about this man's statements and why he was telling me these things. I knew I was saved. I knew I was sealed with the Holy Spirit at the time of my baptism. It really was a remarkable experience.

I was led to ask the pastor about what I should be aware of. I recalled somewhere at sometime hearing a verse of scripture that said to beware of sheep in wolves' clothing or wolves in sheep's clothing. The pastor jumped up, stating, "No! Beware of the men in long trench coats. They preach doom on the street corners; they are false prophets." I didn't know what to believe and kept praying to God for help and protection. I got my answer from prayer when the pastor got up to leave. He looked at me with a fearful look. He then picked up his own long trench coat and hurried out the door. I completely lost faith in that church.

I went out every day and began meeting different people. At times, I still felt that I lugged with me guilt and remorse, as well as fear and shame. These negative emotions opposed my hope of surviving the beginnings of my new life. My fragile hope was sometimes like an elusive wind, blowing on a candle within my heart, mind, and soul. I met a man named Charlie, who said to me, "Go to the mirror, and forgive that man."

Each night, I went to the mirror and said to the image, "I forgive you." But these words rang empty in my ears. I felt so alone. The tormenting loneliness was offset by finding other people with whom to talk. I always found some comfort of belonging and a little peace when talking with others. On another occasion, I was told by a man to stop being so serious about everything and have some fun. I thought it was a wonderful idea, but I did not know how to do that. I was bewildered by that fact until I was invited to a dance.

Understanding a Smile

I watched people dance all night. They smiled and hugged like it was a wonderful celebration. I smiled a lot while watching them dance. I was too scared to ask any of the girls to dance. I found joy in just watching everyone having fun.

After the dance, I returned home to face my image in the mirror. I stood, looking at the image. This time as I looked into my own eyes, I felt something was different. I saw a twinkle of light as I watched the image say, "You are going to be okay." Tears flowed down my cheeks, as I went down on my knees to thank God. I thanked Him that I saw and felt a change.

The following day, I met with a few people who were at the dance. I complained about my face, which hurt. One of them said, "Kurt, you were smiling all last night during the dance. It takes fourteen muscles to smile and seventy-two muscles to frown. You have been exercising the unused muscles in your face."

Later, I got a call from Jerome, a guy I had met once at the local soup kitchen. He used to go there to help others. He told me about a man named Ed, someone I needed to meet. Jerome said I should go see him about my recurring hopelessness. I followed the directions Jerome gave me and arrived at Ed's home. Ed became my first human relations mentor. Ed gave me such wisdom; he began to break down my walls of fear and misunderstanding.

My reality changed when someone cared about my life. The first thing Ed ever said to me was, "You don't have to die. Someone already has." Ed asked me if I wanted a whole new life and to be a free man. He smiled and handed me a book. The book was about twenty-four elders he called living principles. Ed said, "Twelve of these principles will teach you how to find a spiritual life, and the other twelve will help you live in a spiritual place."

Ed called the spiritual society I was invited into the everlasting gospel. He said, "Within these pages, you will find a message about a gift of love." He talked about it as a golden book of revelations. Ed constantly talked about unconditional love. He often suggested ways to do loving and caring things. Every visit to see Ed ensured my grasp on this invitation for a whole new life.

What became most important were Ed's instructions on how to read and study each principle. He said I was to read about each principle for ten days. He would often say, "Stay within the little book." Or, "Do not go outside the kingdom." I visited with him as often as I could. His simple wisdom always brought me the sense of feeling comforted. Ed often suggested I help someone else. "Go have fellowship with others. You have no comprehension of the love of God and man. Go teach what you need to learn. Use your new hope, and tell others about it."

Ed would read to me and tell me stories. His helpmate, Leslie, also showed me considerable kindness when I visited them. They had me over for dinner on several occasions. I actually felt Ed and Leslie's home was like none I had ever known.

The understanding of the light finally came when I found the courage to tell Ed and Leslie about my car accident. I had kept it a secret for almost ten years. Ed talked to me about life after death. After sharing my fear, I felt a new freedom no one else would understand. The hope I had found now revealed a faith, and that faith offered me a chance to know unconditional love. I wanted to share with others the way Ed and Leslie were sharing with me. Leslie asked me, "How are you going to learn about having a relationship unless you go have relationships with other people?"

Ed said to me, "One of these days, I will teach you how to read and write." This made me stop seeing them for a while. I did not believe I had to learn how to read and write. I did not believe I was actually illiterate. I soon found out otherwise.

Searching for Hope

I departed Ed and Leslie's in favor of searching for more of the truth. It was the beginning of a summer that brought with it a welcome twist of fate. I was no longer in the bondage of a life that was helpless, hopeless, and useless. I wanted to experience a greater sense of this new freedom. I had lost my contact with nature as a result of my abuse, and my newfound desire was to be back out in nature. Even as a child, I could find great peace of mind in the wilderness of nature.

One particular summer day, I took a drive out of town. I drove about twenty-five miles before I stopped at a country store. I stepped out of my car to go inside, and I saw a very beautiful woman. She was standing at the edge of the parking lot. Our eyes met, and I felt a shock of embarrassment that I was glaring at her. I turned quickly and entered the country store. But, I held onto the notion that she was a very lovely woman. I whispered a thank you to God for the vision and said a prayer that I might see her again.

When I came out of the store, she was gone. I decided to visit a community health center in the town of Belgrade, Maine. I had heard about this place and that it might have some information to help me. It was absolutely necessary for me to get information to help my health. Not sleeping right and poor eating habits had created emotional turmoil, and I still searched for a better way to live.

I was at the health center, talking with a few people about eating habits, when I heard a very soft voice that grabbed my heart. I looked over to see the same woman who had been outside the country store.

I was captivated by her beauty, and it was all I could do to stay composed. I felt a nervous trembling between wanting to tell her she was very attractive and running away. I admired her for the moment and then left quickly. I was upset with myself, because I saw her as someone so lovely, but I was not good enough to talk with her. She wouldn't care if I thought she was attractive. I went to my car and drove away. She certainly left a wonderful impression upon my mind.

Time passed, and her image was still present in my consciousness. I was afraid of my thoughts and feelings toward her. I pushed my thoughts of her out of my mind. It was weeks later that another trip out to the health center was necessary. I needed to get more information about my poor eating habits. It was a complete surprise to enter the health center and find that same beautiful woman. I sat to calm my sudden nervousness. I was awestruck to look at her and amazed at the light's radiance around her. After a few moments, she walked across the room. I wanted her to know I was looking. I wanted her to know I thought she was beautiful. She didn't notice me sitting there, wanting to get her attention. I began to feel deeply disappointed. A few more moments passed, and I was placed on the spot. After I had lost all hope, she began walking toward me. Our eyes met, and this time she looked away. I thought, *Oh my God, here she comes!*

I tried to compose myself enough to just say hello. She looked straight into my eyes with a bright smile and twinkling eyes. In a soft whispering voice, she said, "Hello there."

I peered sharply into her deep blue eyes and was captured in the wonder of the gleam I saw. "Hello" was all I could say, as I was immediately overwhelmed. I felt something familiar in the light of her eyes and in the kindness I felt from her voice. Something was so familiar yet bewildering. I felt a sudden warmth, and I wanted to leave the place. I did not understand the light and comfort in the warmth I experienced. My subconscious said it was familiar, while my ego said I had better stay away.

I sat in my car outside of the health center, wondering why I was so afraid and confused. Why was she such an attraction? What made me want to tell her she was absolutely lovely? She came out the door and walked toward her car. I was desperate to say something before she left. "Hey!" I yelled. "May I say something to you?" She walked over to me, and I blurted out that there was something I needed to talk about with her. "Will you meet me for a cup of coffee at the cafe across the street?"

"Sure," came softly as her response, and I began to tremble. Why did I ask her to go have coffee? Was it because she was beautiful, and I wanted her to know it? Why didn't I just say that? I held my breath for a moment, as she went to her car and drove across the street to the cafe. I followed her, and we walked in together. We sat in a booth at the Sunset Grill Cafe.

I was extremely nervous and told her that I was. She said, "Yes, me too! I don't quite understand why I agreed to come here with you."

I introduced myself to her. I found her name to be just as lovely as her appearance: Karen echoed into my memory. I said to her, "Karen, I believe that until I say this to you, I will remain uncomfortable." She listened carefully as I began to tell her that I thought she was a beautiful and very attractive woman. "It is only my intention to say to you that you are, and a very disappointing part of my life is being realized. For a very long time, I have not loved or been kind to anyone. I do not know how to, and I have no friends. Love and kindness are very difficult words to say, and do."

"I know," she said. "It is like that with me too."

Karen and I enjoyed the short time we spent together at the cafe. I really enjoyed her smiles and laughter as I told her briefly about myself. She and I departed with no commitment to meet each other again. We just hinted at the suggestion that the health center was someplace we might meet again. Karen was long gone before I wondered why I didn't ask for her telephone number. Oh yes, she was married, and her husband was always away. Something was wrong with her marriage. She was alone a lot and wanted a friend as well. After talking with Karen and finding we had things in common, she was always on my mind. I decided to go to the health center to see if I could find her there. I couldn't believe what I was feeling as I drove my car into the parking lot and found her vehicle. I sat in my car, wondering what I would say and waited for her to come out.

When she did, there was a big smile on her face. Karen told me that she was hoping I would come. I told Karen that she was the only reason I had come. We sat in the parking lot for a couple of hours and talked. We were amazed that we felt the same. During the time we talked, I mentioned again how beautiful she was, and her response brought me that warm feeling of comfort. I was amazed I would say such things. I could never do it before without a drink. I grew a little more comfortable with the feelings I had when I was with her. We exchanged telephone numbers and agreed to talk again. I enjoyed meeting, talking, and eating lunch with her. I began to believe that love really existed and might be found again someday. I told her something was wrong with her husband if he did not want to be with her. He was always away. She feared he was with another woman.

One night, I got a call from Karen. She told me that she had confronted her husband, and he had been with another woman. Karen was very upset and was leaving him to go to her mother's for a while. The next morning, I got another call from Karen. She said her husband had had an accident after she left and was killed. I felt responsible, without reason, and had no more contact with Karen for a while after this tragic news.

A Date to Remember

The phone rang one day, and it was Karen. She had a voice that sounded like a million angels saying, "Hello," straight into my heart. Karen was glad to reach me, and I was happy she called. We both laughed about the same fears that had deferred our hope to talk after the tragedy. We spoke to each other until a beautiful sense of calm came to us. She invited me to come over to her home for coffee. I fell on the couch in disbelief that this beautiful woman had actually invited me to her house. I sat there for a moment, still holding the phone receiver to my ear. I thought about God, *You really are doing for me what I can't do for myself.*

My mind raced as I got ready to go. I was excited to have this opportunity. I had a difficult time staying within the speed limit as I drove to her house, about twenty miles away. As each mile passed, I remained focused on finding a set of stone pillars that marked the turnoff from the main road. I was very uptight and anxious. I was constantly reminding myself to just relax. Once I found the turnoff, a sense of calm came over me. I slowed the car to a near crawl and scanned the distant edge of the headlights. I searched for a little red house on the right side of the road. As each house was examined, my heart pounded with anticipation. Unfamiliar with the road, I circled around and found myself back near its beginning. I lost my excitement as I drove into the woods along the dirt road again. This time, every nook and cranny were examined to find this little red house. It seemed like a long time before my heart jumped and my mind said, *There it is,* and I stopped the car.

I took a few deep breaths as I looked at the red house. Everything felt as though it was in slow motion. I opened the door of my car and stepped out. My mind whispered in the silence of these dark woods, *Go to the door and knock.* The sound of crunching gravel followed me as I approached the house. I paused at the door and waited for total tranquility before I knocked. I looked up at the moon. It was full, glowing beyond the shadow of the huge pine trees. The sound of each knock upon the door was heard echoing off the lake behind the house.

I heard a yell to come in. I walked in to find a little dark-haired boy sitting at the kitchen table. He gave me a smile before looking back over his schoolbooks. "Hello," I said to him.

"My mom will be right out," he said, smiling.

Karen appeared, smiling, and said, "Hello there. This is my son, Jacob," and she smiled at him. "He has homework to do." She tenderly looked at him.

"Hello, Jacob," I said to him again. Looking at Karen, I said, "Hello to you, too, young lady." I could not hide my smile after looking in her lovely blue eyes, which were looking back at me.

Karen began to move around the kitchen and motioned for me to have a seat in the living room. I sat in the living room and watched her move with a gracefulness that was lovely as she made coffee. I was very relaxed and comfortable to just be myself. There was nothing about Karen that threatened me. I was content to be there with her. We spent a few moments talking in the living room before she invited me to see the rest of the house. Karen beamed as she told me how much she appreciated living beside the lake. I asked if we could take a walk outside, and she replied, "Yes, let's go sit on the dock." I paused for a moment, holding my breath and thinking Jacob would object. Karen told him to finish his homework and get to bed. She also told him she and I were going out on the dock to sit and talk. He just smiled and said okay.

It felt risky to find myself doing something I had never taken time to do. In the quiet serenity of the night, we agreed it was nice to be outside and appreciate nature. We whispered back and forth about the full moon and its reflection on the water. The wind blew across the lake and brought the sound of leaves dancing in the trees. There was deep comfort in the mystery of this wonderful night, sitting with Karen beside the lake.

Karen then broke into my comfort zone to say, "Let's go for a boat ride."

"Oh no," I blurted. "I don't know about that. What will the neighbors say?" Then, my fears left, and I said, "Yes, I want to. Are you sure?"

"Sure we can," she replied.

Untying the boat and drifting slowly away from the dock was easy. I gasped at the sound of the motor clanking and roaring. When the motor settled into a soft purr, I relaxed. We headed toward the middle of the lake. The boat slid across the surface of the dark water and into moonlight dancing upon the water. We laughed and smiled, feeling free. The boat motor sputtered to silence as she turned to me and said, "Let's go for a swim."

I boldly said, "Yes, let's. Great idea." Karen had a swimsuit on under her clothes and proceeded to undress at the stern. I stood on the bow, undressing to my boxer shorts. I could vaguely see Karen at the end of the boat. She looked better in her black swimsuit on a white body than I did; in my white boxers, I looked like Casper the Friendly Ghost.

Karen said, "It is cold."

"Don't say that, or I won't go in. Let's just jump on the count of three." We paused before I said, "Ready! 1 … 2 … 3," and we both plunged into the water at the same time. I opened my eyes in total darkness and struggled to get to the surface.

Once at the top, I looked around for Karen and could only see a bright smile and hear a cheerful, "It is wonderful."

"Are you kidding me? It is freezing," I yelled, still gasping for breath. I swam about, trying to generate some body heat, but it was too cold for me. My only resolution was that the sooner I got out, the warmer I would be. We both boarded the boat, and I stood there, shaking like a fragile little bird without feathers. I was embarrassed to be seen so vulnerable and shivering so uncontrollably.

Karen began to chuckle and wrapped a towel around me. I asked for her not to laugh at me, and she said, "Oh no, I understand. This has been wonderful for me. Let's go back to the house and get warm."

"Yes, let's," I said. I sat down and wondered about how good it felt to be alive. We rode silently back to the house. In my heart, I thanked God for allowing me to have this wonderful experience.

After getting warm back at the house, I got up to leave. Karen offered me a hug good-bye, and I couldn't believe a hug was so comforting. I had never felt a hug as nice as the one she gave me. On the way home, I cried tears of joy. I felt alive as I had never before experienced. I had had a prayer answered and found a gift of faith.

Released from Fear

After eight years of working with Pine State Tobacco, I was told that my personality did not fit their philosophy and was fired. I smiled at my former boss, stood, and thanked him before walking out of his office. I was free from the bondage of a job that was no longer satisfying me. A time of change came surprisingly and most unexpectedly, just as meeting Karen had changed my life as well. I went to Ed's house in hope he could help me find the direction I needed to take. I could take the time now to get into school, which was his goal for me. I spent many nights at his home, listening to his spiritual counsel about life. He had a goal for me to get understanding, and that meant getting some education. Ed often said, "One of these days, I will teach you to read and write." He pointed me toward attending school as the direction I needed to take.

Later that day, I called Karen, and she invited me to dinner. Karen couldn't understand how I was able to hide the fact I was illiterate. Karen didn't know she was the first person to whom I had begun to open up to. I had lived most of my life withdrawing from others and hiding my feelings with silence. It was just a short time before all this that the Grace of God had set me free from the bondage of alcohol. Learning to be honest made me ask her for some time to talk together. I loved the gift of voice, and with her, I spoke freely and constantly, sometimes too much.

Karen was someone to talk with: a gift of a friend when I needed a friend. I liked her smiles and laughter, as I told her about my crazy life. Everything seemed easy to talk about with Karen. At dinner,

I told her about wanting to become a writer and a photographer. These two interests were newly found dreams I had when I began asking what I wanted to do with my new life. After becoming sober, I had been taking lots of photographs. I also began wishing I could write captions telling of my feelings about them. I needed to learn to write about those feelings in my voice. Ed had spoken to me several times about the Gifts of God: choice, voice, vision, feeling, and manifestation. These gifts were to support the spiritual way of living I would get from following the twenty-four spiritual principles he suggested were a good design for spiritual living.

I discovered I also wanted to learn to love and be loved. I would struggle sometimes to approach Karen and talk. When I talked too much, I expressed what had happened to me in life because I was ignorant, meaning unlearned in the truth about living by spiritual principles and illiterate, meaning unable to read, write, and comprehend. It hurt Karen to understand this still hurt and limited me. Her sadness would upset me. I know sadness and grief as though they are my best friends. We both had our own forms of grief. I knew she had grief over the loss of her husband. We both suffered losses in the way we were living.

With each attempt to fill out a job application, it became obvious that my lack of any literacy skills would make my job search futile. Finally, the day arrived to seek professional help for my literacy problem. I found going to the college brought a bright promise and new meaning. This new hope was soon dashed, when the clerk in the enrollment office handed me some applications to fill out. I sat at the table, staring at the questions. I had the pencil clutched in my hand, and I saw words that meant nothing. I scrunched up the application and tossed it into the trash can on my way out the door. *What am I going to do?* plagued my mind. I was restless, irritable, and discontented. I was alone and afraid, jobless, and broke while I waited for unemployment benefits which I never questioned getting because I had been fired. There was no appeal when I signed up for unemployment.

Finding help was an unmerciful time of struggle. The clerk at the food stamp office frowned when she had to ask about answers I had put on that application. They were unreadable to her. The clerk smiled and apologized that I was not qualified for food stamps. This made me angry and confused, and I lost faith that my life would get any better. The clerk at the food stamp office also remarked that there were millions of dollars available to the poor. I wondered why I was with such false hope to kill the hunger pangs I had acquired in the last few days.

The next day, I visited the soup kitchen for something to eat. It was there that I found the motivation and courage to go back to the college and try again. After being served something to eat, I wiped away the tear that slid down my face. I remembered what Ed had said about needing school. I did not want to join company with the hungry and homeless at the soup kitchen. I decided to go up to the college.

Dying to Learn

I embarked on a mission to the college with a new understanding of what I had to admit. I was handed the application forms to fill out, as I stood in front of the clerk's desk. This time, I did not scrunch up the application for the wastebasket. Another woman came out from her office and saw me standing there, my head hung in shame. She cheerfully asked me, "Young man, may I help you?"

I looked up at her as my insides began to tremble, and my eyes welled with tears. "I cannot read and write. I need to come to school and learn, but I cannot even fill out this application."

"Oh, I understand." She smiled at me and cheerfully invited me to come into her office, where she would help me. She said, "Kurt, you're not alone. There are lots of men out there just like you, who cannot read and write."

She read me the questions on the admissions form and explained what they were asking. She wrote my answers, while I wiped away my tears of shame. Once the forms were complete, she told me of a skills testing date. She asked me to attend, and I agreed—with apprehension.

On the day of the skills test, I had my hand on the classroom door, wondering how I had ever gotten through school. I had a diploma but could not read or write. My first job was meeting Bret at the bar and there was no application. My second was a handshake after talking with the general manager of Pine State. After the test results came back, I was allowed to enroll in the basic reading and writing classes. I clung to the hope of believing that I was on the right path.

Once I made the admission that I was illiterate, my journey out of the darkness had a brighter horizon. The priceless joy of my life came with the opportunity to change. I proceeded with my desire to find fulfillment in a better life. Karen was a good listener, and I enjoyed telling her about the promises of the bright future I began to see on the horizon. I grew to care about my life more and more. I would call Karen on the phone and tell her what my writing lessons were. I would practice reading with her.

At school, I was asked to write an essay for my final in writing class. I was asked to do a book report for my final in my reading class. I was embarrassed at not have anything about which to write. I was told to write about something I knew how to do, so I decided to write about the first time I got drunk. I knew how to drink. I wrote about drinking for the first time at the high school dance.

The teacher came to me after the assignment and asked me a strange question. "Kurt, what do you think you deserve for a grade on your essay final?"

I said, "I deserve an A."

Surprised, she asked, "Why?" I told her that when I began class, I could not write a sentence. And, by attending classes she taught, I could now write sentences, put together a paragraph, and write that essay. I received an A in Basic Writing 101.

The book report in my reading class was also a challenge. I had no clue what book to read. I chose to read and report on *The Big Book of Alcoholics Anonymous*. I read it and did my book report. I received an A and a note from the teacher, saying I could have picked an easier book. I remembered Ed and what he had said about the little book of twenty-four principles he had given me. I decided to read each principle for ten days. I would call Karen and practice reading.

I loved that I could now read and write. This opened up a whole new world of being able to understand and comprehend a spiritual way of life. I read the little book, and it was sweet to read. But, it also made my belly bitter to the point I had to puke the vile manifestation of darkness inside me. The third and fourth principles had me amazed before I was halfway through. You don't have a chance unless God steps in was principle 3, and unless I did principle 4, tell my story, I would die of my secrets. My life went from the darkness of death toward the light of living. I found the gift of love. I believed Ed when he called it the everlasting good news of unconditional love. I began to write poetry and loved reading my poems to Karen. One day, she mentioned that I ought to get my poems published. It became a dream, as I began to consider getting published.

Dreams Reborn

I had met Karen in June, and December was now arriving. The time that had passed showed me how my lack of responsibility had cost me the affections of my family. Karen had much stronger relations with her family, and I admired that about her. Christmastime became a big distraction. I began to spend less time with Karen, as she spent more time with her family. I felt awkward, as Christmas began to form a different meaning in my mind. I called Karen to come over before she left for the holidays. She had plans that would be taking her out of state. My plans were to get through the holidays.

I sat near my window, looking outside. I wondered what to give Karen for Christmas. I wanted her to have something special, something out of the ordinary. I gazed at the snow outside my window, and I thought about making her a snow angel. I got up and went outside to make one. I looked around the neighborhood to make sure no one was watching me. I said, "God, grant me the serenity to accept the things I cannot change. Courage to change the things I can, and wisdom to know the difference." I then lay down to make an angel in the snow. The angel was beautiful, and it was a perfect gift.

When Karen arrived, I could not contain myself and immediately began to tell her I had no money for a gift. I told Karen I wanted her to have the memory of this angel, because she had been one to me. I opened the curtains and watched her smile a smile that was so precious. It melted my heart to see her with a priceless smile. Karen gave me a hug. I still felt a hug was something fearfully wonderful.

Karen began telling me about her family and the Christmases

they had. I was amazed at her excitement. I was bewildered why I was not. My own personal desires seemed so far away with my family. I was considering the idea of calling my family for Christmas. That idea was better than the years I spent drunk during the holidays and had no contact with any of my family. The year before, I was with Ed and Leslie. Christmas was spent at a local church with others who had no family or place to go. Ed and Leslie brought me there and told me I was not alone. I decided I would attend that church again for Christmas.

Christmas morning arrived, and I prepared to leave for church. I stepped out of my apartment onto the porch and found a card stuck in my mailbox. I opened it to find a message from Karen. It said, "My friend, go look outside your window." I ran back up the steps to my living room window. I took a deep breath and pulled back the curtains. There was another angel, which Karen had made beside the one I made for her. My heart burst with joy, and tears streamed down my face as I felt a gift of God's love. From the words, "my friend," I believed the spirit of Christmas entered my heart. I went to church and met with the people gathered for a Christmas dinner. I came to believe on Christmas Day that angels and love really existed.

The New Freedom

What will I do now? was on my mind from time to time after getting fired from Pine State Tobacco. I constantly prayed for help and direction. The telephone rang one day, while I was praying and sitting alone in my apartment. I thought, *An answer is on the way. This may be it.* I moved quickly to answer the phone. It was Jerome, the young man who introduced me to Ed. Jerome spoke to me with excitement! "Hey pal, do you remember that farm we stopped at last summer, the Journeys End? It's down near the river."

"Oh yea," I said.

"Well, I was down there today, and there were six eagles: a pair of bald eagles and two pair of golden eagles. There are some people who placed food out on the frozen river, and the eagles came to visit and eat. You should get your camera and take a ride out. They are beautiful."

Jerome was correct to think I might be interested. He was aware I enjoyed photography and being out in nature. But, I was skeptical about seeing the eagles and didn't pursue the idea of photographing them. Three days passed before my skepticism lost out to the truth that I wouldn't know until I went to see for myself.

A clear blue sky helped brighten my attitude. A fresh new snowfall made it a beautiful winter day to go out and fulfill my desire to take some photographs. It was a twelve-mile trip to the farm by the river.

When I was close, I slowed the car and began to look around for the eagles. I drove slowly, peering into the sky above the farm, out over the fields to the far horizon, and into the woods around the area. I was disappointed there were no signs of any life in the air or on the ground. Suddenly, I began to blink and squint into the glare of near sunset reflecting on the frozen river. A golden path of sunlight lay like a carpet on the ice leading up the river. This would be a good photograph. I parked the car, got out, and soon realized why there were no signs of life.

The bitter cold touched my ears and began zapping them into numbness. My fingers began to complain about the freezing cold temperature of the outside air. I moved to photograph the sunset and was startled as I stepped over the guardrail; I had disturbed a gaggle of geese, hiding under the bridge, the only creatures that dared brave the intense cold. My heart got an unexpected jump-start. The geese loudly told me they were annoyed, and I moved away from them as quickly as I could.

The wind blew briskly against my face, while I moved to the right location for a good photograph. The sun blasted bright orange into my eyes, while I occasionally looked up for the right location. I walked along with my head down, bracing from the wind. I looked up after a short distance and was stopped cold in my tracks. I saw the silhouette of a large bird perched on a limb. I felt a calm serenity with this amazing sight. A beautiful eagle was perched in silhouette within the orange of a setting sun.

I was too far away from the eagle for a good photograph. I stood there in amazement, now unaware that it was bitter cold. Suddenly, the silhouette seemed to fall from the branch, and a much larger bald eagle began to take flight. After a few graceful flaps of its wings, this wonderful eagle slowly soared upward into the sunset. In just a few moments, it was a speck high above the far horizon and gone. I captured the experience in my heart and wondered about the breathtaking amazement of being out alone, standing on a frozen river in winter, and watching this bald eagle fly. The joy of being free filled my heart.

Up on the Mountain

I wanted to write and take photographs. I wanted more of the joy I felt with writing and doing photography.

I found constant motivation when writing. I had the recognition of winning a poetry contest. I sent a poem to a contest and won the honor of an outstanding literary accomplishment. I sent some photos to a contest and won an award. Out of twenty thousand entries in the contest, a photo were in the top one hundred. The only real question I needed to ask myself was what I want to do in life.

The answer was clear, and the time was available to devote to gaining experience. I had no job, no commitments to anyone, and just enough money to take a risk. It was time to take a trip to the mountains to write and take photographs. It was time for action. My own peace of mind rested on how ready I was to go somewhere I had not been and do what I had not done. To do this would provide the experience I lacked.

I packed some clothing and prepared for a trip to Sugarloaf Mountain. I was driven with a desire for change. I departed on my trip with peace of mind, and I was happy. Sugarloaf Mountain was two hours away. Along the road up to the mountain, a crystal-clear stream glittered with the sunlight's reflection as it flowed. The road turned upward and away from the glittering stream, and Sugarloaf Mountain was in sight. I was excited and glad I had come this far in my endeavor to find contentment and to do something I loved. I was reaching for a new pinnacle in the joy of living.

Sugarloaf Mountain rose high above me, directly in the frame of my car's windshield. I felt inspired to see such beauty as I traveled toward my final destination. Driving along, I came to the hotel where I would spend the night. I parked the car and began admiring the huge white thunderhead clouds billowing near the peak of this magnificent mountain. There certainly was the feeling of a presence of some great inspiration and mystery. The wind blew briskly through the trees and created sounds like a whispering song. The song ended as I walked into the resort hotel.

I entered my hotel room after checking in, and it was dead quiet. The room came to life when the lights came on and the bathwater started bubbling in the tub. I wanted to have a relaxing hot bath after my long drive. After a hot bath, it did not take long to drift off to sleep on the room's big soft bed. I had a dream about some woman I sought. I awoke suddenly, my stomach growling. I wanted to love, and the love I needed at this time was food. Perhaps the woman in the dream was my mother. Before we became so estranged, she was the only woman I knew who would remind me to eat.

I took a short walk in the late summer sunset to the hotel dining room. I became overwhelmed when entering the dining room and seeing that one entire wall was a window. Outside this window was the view of a nearby valley. From across the distance came a sheet of dark clouds. The clouds arrived with the darkness of the coming night. I ate a nice dinner and returned to my room. It was not long that I, too, was visited by the darkness of sleep.

I was up at sunrise after some very precious rest. The morning sun was beaming down one side of the mountain. Clouds cast gloomy shadows upon the face of the mountain. The clouds seemed to be racing along on their own secret journey to form some important purpose elsewhere. I walked toward the dining room for breakfast. It became clear that a hike up the mountain would be great for taking photographs.

The dining room held more people than the previous night. Lots of greetings were given and received. Smiles and laughter filled the room. I sat near the big picture window and was awestruck by the natural beauty of this majestic place. There were many shades of green that bearded the smaller mountains around this valley. The evergreen trees were a beautiful mask. Breakfast was served buffet style. Ham, bacon, eggs, juice, coffee, and an assortment of sliced fruits seemed to be a banquet for a king.

After breakfast, I went outside. The sky held its own bounty of white clouds of different shapes and sizes; streams of golden warm sunshine fell between them. I prepared my camera and started walking into the woods. I followed a rocky path and, after a short distance, emerged into a clearing. I was just above tree level on the mountain slope and, looking behind me, had my first photograph. I advanced upward toward another view, and soon, the whole valley was in front of me. Another photograph showed the changed scene, and my attitude also changed. I begin a much harder climb up the mountain slope. It was a slow climb, however, and the birds telling each other of my presence gave me a distraction. Smiling, I took another photograph after reaching a higher perspective. I looked up toward the peak of the mountain as clouds were gathering to cover it, and my hope of a pinnacle view was lost.

I was a little tired and considered this a turning point. I saw a broken ski pole. It would help me reach a higher position on the mountain. My pants were soggy, and my feet got colder as the morning dew of the grass was absorbed into them. I was not much for mountain climbing.

A piece of foam from a glove was another discovery. The foam fit on the end of the broken ski pole, providing perfect support as one person's trash turned into salvaged treasure—a treasure to build confidence for the success in this climb up Sugarloaf Mountain.

Nearly halfway up the mountain slope, it was time to rest. I went off the trail to a cut tree stump. A place to sit on this slope was like a seat of mercy. Fresh air, sunshine, and quiet serenity began my thanks to God. A breeze blowing down the mountain sounded like a sweet, relaxing song. It felt so wonderful to obtain the peace I expected to find at the top.

I spent a few more moments observing the scenery before beginning my adventure back down the mountain. Looking around with curiosity, something caught my attention. There were little red spots in the grass. Sliding down to look closer revealed wild strawberries. I picked a handful to eat, stood up, and was ready to walk down the mountain. I met other people on their way up, and I was glad to tell them about the wild strawberries. I called that my joy and a victory. There was no disappointment in not reaching the pinnacle. In the valley, I heard the sounds of church bells. There was peace there for today. I had found a deep peace within myself.

Going Backward to Move Forward

Learning to pray for God's will was a gift. God gave me hope and love with Ed and faith and love with Karen. Finding the two angels on Christmas Day and the eagle reminded me of the freedom to feel loved. The mountain was a place where I found peace. Learning to read and write gave me courage. Knowing God and discovering His will had become a joy.

I came back from the mountain and went to see Ed. My visit with him was quite disturbing in two ways. Ed revealed to me the seriousness of having made a contract with Satan. To have vowed to never love again after getting so hurt. To agree with the prince of darkness that I would not love if he would not harm Kelly. This was something I never told Ed about, so I knew God's spirit was addressing me personally through him. I was on my way out the door after the visit when he remarked that my troubles with Karen were related to my car accident. At that time, I did not understand what he meant, but I clearly understood his comment about the contract. After I returned to my apartment, I decided I wanted to move away from Maine.

Before leaving Maine, I submitted my poetry for copyright. I was feeling the desire Karen had about getting them published. The dream now seemed worthwhile. I sent a manuscript to a publisher in Boston. They replied with a rejection letter, saying they had no market for my book. They wanted work about devil worship, goddess spirituality, and pagan theology. There was no place in their market for my work. I laughed, saying aloud after reading the letter, "God, what is this?"

I got my answer: "Well, Kurt, you know what it is not." I was relieved to know it was not devil worship, goddess spirituality, or pagan theology.

I gave up the dream of being published. Now, I was really done with life in Maine and ready to find greener pastures. I had no fear that I could not live in a different state. I considered going to the Grand Canyon too.

I wanted to stop along the way and see Kelly in Maryland. I left Maine and arrived in Maryland. I found out where Kelly lived and went to visit her. She was receptive to the fact that it was better for me to quit drinking than to go on like I had been. I discovered something I did not know while apologizing to her. Kelly revealed to me the abortion she had was not of my child. She admitted she had an affair with some guy when we were having trouble. I found that my primary purpose to have been such a drunkard and a disappointment to Kelly was to take responsibility for my part in our relationship and forgive her.

After my visit with Kelly, I took some time to find Bret at the swimming pool company in Rockville. I visited Bret and a few others who still worked there. They were quite happy I had stopped drinking. Bret, Sam, Fred, and Willy congratulated me on my success in staying sober. But, the other two men, Dennis and Kevin, were not impressed. Dennis asked me when I had last got slapped. I considered his question as a pretty sad way to be remembered. I was the guy who got slapped across the face by the waitress at the Bitter Lemon Pub. Kevin wanted to remind me about Mr. Banks' pool. Kevin was who I lied to that caused me to get fired. Mr. Banks was a war veteran, who had a service contract with the pool company. It was my job to visit his home once a week and ensure that the pool was maintained. I never saw Mr. Banks and began skipping his service. Mr. Banks called Kevin one day and wanted to know why the pool was green. Mr. Banks was having a party and was upset his pool was pea green. When I arrived back at the office, Kevin asked me if I had serviced Mr. Banks' pool. I said, "Yes."

He said, "You're a liar. The pool is green, and they want to have a pool party this weekend." I got fired from the pool company the next day. Finding out about Kelly's affair was very disenchanting; listening to Dennis remember me as the guy who got slapped and hearing Kevin tell the tale of me getting fired over Mr. Banks' pool was a lesson in humility.

I spent a week in the area, remembering a lot more of my old drinking life. Now that I was not drinking myself into oblivion, it became clear I had much more work to do. More work than a few simple and casual apologies. What could I do to make restitution for harms done to people and the damages I did to places and things? It was painful to remember how I had tried to find my way through life as a drunk, lost in the darkness. I recalled the destruction during the last days of drinking at the beach, which constituted my last bender. I went back to the beach with the hope of making restitution. I had a dream of wanting to live at the beach. I had a desire to change.

I began my life in Ocean City, Maryland. Shortly after arriving, my mission was to go to the place in Gaithersburg, Maryland, where I had made the deal with Satan. I went to the place behind the Silver Fox Tavern, where I had overdosed and got down on my knees. I asked Jesus to forgive what I had done. I prayed He would cover me with His blood and break the contract. I cried in sorrow that I did not know Him. I got up off my knees and returned to the beach in Ocean City.

Loving and enjoying life now seemed unavoidable. A camera and pen helped create some finer moments in living my new life at the beach. I visited the police department on arriving back in town. I offered them an apology with gratitude. I could now appreciate them for having done their job one night when they found me drunk on the boardwalk. They appeared puzzled at first when I said, "Thanks for beating me up on the boardwalk." They looked relieved when I said, "It caused me to get help and stop drinking." It was nice to depart the police department with them smiling at me.

Doing the next right thing found me experiencing the next reward. I was walking down the street and saw a police officer. The police officer was walking toward me. I did not flinch with fear, and I had no desire to cross the street. I just continued with my purpose: enjoying my walk down the street. The police officer looked at me, and I looked at him as we passed each other. His remark, "Good afternoon, sir," made me pause. I looked back as he continued walking and thought, *That was nice. He called me sir. He did not say, "Stop, you're under arrest," or, "You have the right to remain silent." He said, "Good afternoon, sir."* I appreciated that moment of respect.

New Life at the Beach

I got a room at a rooming house and began looking for work. My first job application was successfully completed. It was amazing to hear the man say, "You're hired," though not because I had experience to do the work. He had a smile on his face that I had filled out the job application correctly. He said, "See this little gray box on the application? You're the first person not to write something in it."

I said, "Well, it says, 'Do not write in this box.'"

He chuckled and said, "Yes, and you're the first person not to write in it. I have taken a lot of applications, and most people write in it." What a gift to have been able to read!

Wally befriended me as a teaching employer. He was always willing to show me how to do the work and then let me go at it. Wally was a compassionate mentor. He was always smiling and very pleased that I showed up for work every day. The others who worked for him added stress because of their drinking. Wally would often remark to me about it. For many, life at this beach resort/restaurant/ nightclub was just a party. I often received raises and praise for the job I did. Learning from Wally was a pleasure.

I learned carpentry skills, plumbing skills, and landscaping. These were all part of my daily activities at the hot spot resort restaurant/ nightclub called Secrets. I became a better maintenance man after Chris got fired, which revealed what drinking can do to a man. Chris became a bitter rival for his own job security. He pressed me like a thorn, when it was obvious he drank way too much. Chris seemed always to appear fearful of why I did not drink. His boasting and bragging often made others, as well as me, turn away.

One morning, Chris called me to help him catch up on his work. I was not done with my own work. Chris kept shouting, and finally, Jeff, a third man just hired for maintenance, came to see his dilemma. It was just another hangover slowing Chris's work. When I arrived, Chris was really upset. I chuckled at a comment Jeff made; Jeff who was all too eager to badger Chris about his complaining.

Chris's bloodshot eyes rested upon me, and a startling comment came out of his mouth. "See that knife there?" he asked as he pointed to a small kitchen knife sticking in a nearby tabletop. "I ought to stick you with it." His alcohol breath was now in my face. I stepped back and looked at this poor, pathetic, broken spirit. I had seen a similar reflection in my mirror, when I was drinking myself to death. I knew he was bluffing and mainly crying out for help. I said a quick prayer and a promise I had heard ran through my mind: keep on the firing line of life, and God will keep you protected.

Chris's provocation could not be taken lightly. Looking directly into his soulless eyes, I boldly said, "Go ahead. I am standing right here, Chris!" He stepped back, disappointed that I had called his bluff.

He said, "That's what I hate about you. You're not scared of anything." Chris then walked away. Jeff was shocked that I said what I did, but I knew he did not know what I knew about someone suffering like Chris.

Jeff reported Chris's conduct to Wally. Wally asked me if I was okay. I said, "Yes, Chris just had too much to drink last night." I returned to work the following day and discovered that Chris had been fired. He was getting drunk after work and mouthing off to another employee, a bartender who went directly to the owner.

It was late in early spring when Jeff came to me, asking if I would work for him the following day. I had been working a six-day, ten-hour-a-day routine for two months. It was supposed to be my day off, but I said yes. Soon after, Jeff s gratitude was forgotten, and I realized it was not what I really wanted to do. My own greed began to bother me.

I was not paying attention to what I was doing, set down a chair, and pinched my finger. A bloody gash had me struggling to complete the day's work. A Band-Aid covered the wound, and I went home. Early the next morning, I awoke with a throbbing finger. My finger screamed in pain when touched. I kept my promise to Jeff that I would work the next day, and I went to work despite being wounded. I had three hours before the place opened. I swept and washed the floors. My finger had me cussing when I touched the chairs. Pain rocketed up my wrist, when I was not being careful when handling them.

It was taking me longer to do my work because of the injury to my finger. I kept murmuring from the pain of contact between my finger and the chairs. The floor was swept and washed clean. The tables and chairs were set up in the dining room before I moved into the bar area. The bar smelled of stale beer and like death had visited the night before; it reminded me of once upon a time in my past. Pushing the mop around the barroom was difficult.

I heard a strange, soft, scratching and fluttering noise. I continued working until I heard it again. "What is that?" I asked myself while walking around the bar. Suddenly, the noises directed me to a little sparrow trapped in a corner of the window. "Oh," I said, and the hope of making a rescue moved me toward the little bird. I soon discovered it was not willing to be caught so easily. The sparrow hopped over each attempt to catch him, and I chuckled at my efforts to capture him with one hand. I dismissed my throbbing finger to cradle the little bird with both hands. I was surprised the sparrow became so calm after I captured him.

I looked at him and thought, *What are you doing in here?* Looking into his eyes, they seemed to say, "Let me go free please!" *Oh yes, it will be an honor to let you go free after catching you,* I thought. I walked out on the deck and looked into the clear blue sky. I tossed the tiny sparrow. He shot away like an arrow. Walking back into the bar, my eyes welled with tears. "Lord, why am I crying?" My thoughts were about being free to go home soon as well.

Now quite cheerful, the time flew by, and I was on my way home. In my room later that night, I heard my name called. I dismissed it. I heard my name called again. I felt something like a tap on my shoulder. I turned around, and no one was there. I heard my name called again, and leaning back in my chair, I heard a soft whisper in my ear. "Listen!" I looked behind me, and no one was there. A soft voice said, "Remember the little sparrow you set free from the bar this morning?"

"Yes," I replied.

"Well, that was you almost four years ago, trapped in a barroom."

Helping Others

Away from my work at Secrets, my time was spent writing poetry and taking photographs. I enjoyed the gifts of voice and vision and the abilities to see, hear, and feel with these gifts. I met a young man named Harry one day. Harry had also just moved to the beach. We had a brief meeting on the boardwalk, where we shared the bench at first as strangers. Harry broke the ice first, commenting that he was miserable about his drinking. The misery Harry spoke of sounded so familiar. He was miserable and questioning whether not drinking was worth it. I believe our meeting to be a divine setup because of the way it occurred. I no longer spoke with Harry as a stranger about understanding his dreadful condition. I talked, and he listened. After our brief conversation, Harry left me sitting on the bench. I did not mind being a benchwarmer, as I prayed to God that Harry would find a faith that worked for him.

It was interesting how many times Harry appeared in my life after our first meeting. We would "accidentally" meet up on the boardwalk. Harry was still seeking help to get over his spiritual malady: the soul sickness that was a consequence of his obsession for alcohol and drugs. Harry showed interest in a solution and was excited when I offered to help.

I was walking along the beach with Harry and abruptly stopped. I looked at him and asked, "You really want help with your life?"

He looked at me with a desperate face. "Yes, for one thing, I want to know why you're smiling all the time, and why you don't drink."

I looked at the beach and out over the ocean and said to him,

"Harry, see that ocean? Do you believe it is more powerful than you are? Do you believe God created that ocean?"

Harry answered, "Yes!"

"Well, let me introduce you to my God, who is all powerful." I invited Harry to kneel right there on the boardwalk. Harry and I both knelt, and I asked Harry to repeat this prayer with me: "God, I offer myself to thee, to do with me and build with me as thou will. Relieve me of the bondage of self that I may better do thy will. Take away my difficulties that stand in the way of my usefulness to you and my fellows. Thy will, not mine, be done." We stood together, and I said to Harry, "That's it. The hardest part is done. If you believe me now, there is a book of twenty-four principles I want you to read." I talked to him about Ed, a gift of love, and the ten-day plan.

Harry and I began meeting every day, and I would read to him or listen as he read. Harry often came with stories about how his life was changing and that God's grace was responsible for the change. I found a true joy in my heart the day Harry finally cracked a joke about himself. We both laughed at the insanity of what addiction can do to a person. Harry was undergoing a profound change of life using the same twenty-four principles I had practiced. Twelve helped us stay spiritually fit and twelve helped us live in a spiritual society. It was time to let Harry go and do what he did not believe he could do.

I said, "Go help someone else. I will be around." Just as Ed had said and done with me, I said and did with Harry. And it worked. From the words of a great man came a wise saying: "Freely ye have received, freely give." There is no greater love than a man laying down his life for another.

A Dream Comes to Pass

Living near the ocean, I enjoyed life each day. And just when I thought it couldn't get better, it did. One day, I received a letter from a publisher in Pittsburgh. Pittsburgh was where I had had my last drink, and that was all I knew about it. Dorrance Publishing Company sent me a letter offering the opportunity for my poetry to be shared with the reading public. I reconsidered my dream of getting published and discovered I had nothing to lose. I knew I wanted to share the book of poems, because I was told I could not be a writer. So, I agreed to have a book of seventy-two poems published.

I wanted to share it as a gift I had been given. I was excited and began working toward my goal of becoming a published author. The released book brought priceless gifts. My first royalty check arrived and covered my apartment's electric bill. I was amazed that my efforts to put words on paper now provided me with comfort.

The most profound experience with the book was not the autograph parties or the newspaper articles. My best gift was meeting with a man one day who told me God had lifted his obsession with drugs. After he spoke, I gave him a book of my poetry. "I want you to have this book," I said, and I told him enough about my freedom from addiction for him to understand the power of God's love.

About a month later, I was at a store and heard someone call my name. I turned to see a man running toward me. I didn't recognize him at first. He hugged me, and tears streamed down his face. I began to tremble after his embrace as he said, "Kurt, I took your little book down to the men's meeting at our church. We were studying the book of Ephesians about putting on the armor of God! One of your poems helped me understand scripture."

I nodded, and all I could say was, "It has nothing to do with me." I thanked him and left quickly, kind of puzzled about what he said. I drove away, and tears began streaming down my face. I said, "God, what are you doing? I wrote those poems a few years ago for Karen, and you're telling me it helped this man understand scripture?"

I heard my name spoken clearly in my heart. "Kurt, you have no idea what I am going to do with you." At that moment, I felt a pat on the back, like a "well done." It seemed like all the oh nos I had done all my life were washed away with this one "That a boy." I felt a strong joy that made me cry and laugh so loudly that driving became impossible. I had to pull over to the side of the road and breathe until I was calm.

My mind began to open into a deeper spiritual understanding. I continued to try to live as a human being with the gift of love. The reality of a heaven and a hell were becoming less foggy. I engaged in relationships with other people. Spiritual, emotional, mental, and physical were all new and exciting aspects to consider when having personal relations with others. I befriended an old man named Jack, after finding him to be bold like Ed. He was bold enough to confront me with his own wisdom about the love of God. Jack became a friend, and over a few years before his death, he helped me a lot.

The Power of Loneliness

Jack's death left me lonely. I had grown to love and care for him as my friend. I grieved like I never had when I lost my childhood friends. I thought of a solution and sent my prayers to God for a mate. Shelly soon appeared and found a place in my heart. Shelly said, "I hear you have written a book. I would like a copy." Looking at the radiance of her beauty, I was captivated. I wanted to spend time with her and see if she was interested in more than a book.

The conversation with Shelly about my book exposed her secret. Shelly turned out to be a very unhappy woman. She would come and go frequently in my life. She was after her own happiness and a divorce. We met often before the time came for an ultimatum. I had been offered a job in South Carolina, and I met with Shelly to discuss it. I told Shelly that if I were to stay, I eventually wanted to get married. She agreed that eventually we could. She seemed to find happiness with me, and we continued dating.

Shelly was the mother of three beautiful children. Recently divorced, she shared custody with her former husband. I could not see or understand that the years of wanting to save my mother from her problems had given me a need to save myself from the self-pity I felt with the women I got involved with. I wanted to rescue Shelly and her children. I also thought getting married to Shelly was the answer to my feeling alone. This presented us with many challenges. We took the kids camping and fishing. We took them to amusement parks. They were always included in our plans. Whenever they were with their father, Shelly and I embarked on our own thrilling adventures.

It was my deep desire to be a good husband and stepfather to the children. Blessings continued to pour into my life, and I felt I was doing right. Sometimes after returning from work, the children would come running to hug me and ask if I would play. Shelly would sometimes cry when she observed her children's happiness. They would crawl into my lap before bed and beg me to read them a story. Shelly's comment to me after reading to them was, "They cannot even do that with their real father." This caused me to cry while all were asleep. I knew about having a father who was not available.

The hardest part of my marriage to Shelly was my perception of the kids being happy and excited to see their real dad. They would return so damaged and sad. He would spend his time with them drinking. All the promises he had made them were broken. It took a concerted effort from Shelly and I to bring the kids back to joy. At our home, they were happy most of the time. I was having flashbacks of the conflicts unresolved with my mother drinking and my father's broken promises.

Shelly and I thought going to church might help our overall life. We began attendance at a local Baptist church. The year we spent together and the short ninety days of our marriage were soon like a butterfly in a spider's web. The religious implications brought a quick demise to all we had worked for. I came home from work one day, and Shelly said, "I do not believe we are married."

I said, "Honey, I am sure. I was there." She was so upset with me and accused me of deceiving her. She claimed to be in trouble for divorcing her husband and marrying me. She was afraid God would not recognize our marriage, that God would not bless our marriage because she had been a Catholic and was married before. She claimed that the pastor told her we should not have been married by a Methodist minister, and their religion was wrong. I went to the Baptist church and spoke to the pastor. He called Shelly while I was there, and after he hung up the phone, he told me Shelly wanted to reconcile with her first husband. He said I had committed adultery to have married her. I was lost in fear that I had done something wrong. I could not respond to what seemed like mass confusion. So, I just agreed to leave the marriage.

I loved Shelly and accepted what I thought she wanted to be

happy. I was devastated. I felt like someone took a bazooka, put it to my chest, and blew out my heart. I fell to my knees and asked God what to do. "Leave now," was all I heard. I left Shelly after returning from seeing the Baptist preacher. As I walked away, I felt myself in a place of no love.

I visited the pastor of the church again. He said to come to church, and the following Sunday, I did. I was met at the doors of the church by the pastor and told I could not go in. Shelly was in the church with her former husband. He told me they were getting back together. I left church bewildered and found out a little later they were not getting back together. I felt forsaken.

Mending the Fences

Heartbroken, I quit my job at the beach and returned to Maine. I visited my mother, whom I had not seen in years. I had to visit Ed and Leslie. Ed was loud and direct when he said I had married someone just like my mother. "You just wanted someone to take care of you. And you picked a woman who was unable to give you what you wanted." Ed was upset at my behavior and mostly talked to me about absolution and atonement. I felt Ed was telling me the truth.

Extremely heartbroken, I stayed with my mother for a while. I thought God had forsaken me. I came to realize I had married Shelly because I was lonely and wanted someone to take care of me. I thought if I could rescue her she would love me. I realized Kelly, Karen, and Shelly were all relationships I began because I was lonely not because I was in love. I love the creation more than the Creator in each instance. I began smoking heavily. I went from smoking a pack a day to almost three packs a day. I prayed to God for help, but I prayed without faith. I had a deep wound on my soul. I felt my heart would never mend, and my body was in shock over how things had gone between Shelly and myself which eventually ended the relationship.

Soon after I arrived back in Maine, I met another man named Harold. He seemed to come along with a passion for reading the Bible. He, too, was hurt by a marriage gone wrong. Harold and I met each day and constantly searched and read the Bible for a better understanding of God's will. When we were not reading the Bible, we went fishing. I began praying to turn my heart over to God, because all I kept doing was breaking it. I enjoyed reading the Bible and studying God's word. I began watching Trinity Broadcasting every day and night. As defeated as I felt, I began to have a deeper spiritual experience with unconditional love and a more profound awakening.

It was amazing to me to have direct and personal encounters with God. The idea was extremely new to me because of my understanding of God and my religious upbringing. I had thought God was unattainable except by certain elite individuals, otherwise known as clergy.

Satan has brought forth many onslaughts to prevent the Lord's will from manifesting in my life. My desire to seek and do God's will has caused me to have questions about faith. My intellect created the barrier that often gave me limited conclusions of human understanding in spiritual matters. The majesty of having Jesus Christ revealed to me and to see the unfolding of a bigger plan for living left me stunned, with head bowed, and weeping at its beauty. The reading of the Bible released burdens from my mind. The joy of believing creates an awesome feeling of oneness with God, our Father. God's love breaks down the fortress of my emotional human nature, creating a need to trust and pay careful attention to Him.

The discipline needed to experience a change in thinking from ignorance to wisdom is not always met with good cheer. Still, as time passes, it becomes a joy. Praising and worshipping God within my own temple brought this experience and my need of Jesus Christ to be my Lord and Savior.

It was my human weakness to live in a world that rejected Jesus Christ and His message. I now took actions to follow Him that would risk the loss of understanding from my family, my friends, and the world at large. The rewards borne of most of the changes left me confident and assured that He is my Lord and Savior.

Having time to spend in the divine presence of God is granted as a right to the children of God. Most, if not all, earthly responsibilities were removed from my life, except the basic needs to eat and sleep.

A night I will always remember brought the late-night hours to pass with my face pressed into prayers for wisdom. I sought knowledge of God's will. In worship over reading the Bible, I was suddenly in a vision of this bright angelic light. The definition of it as an angel was difficult to determine in such intense light as was shown to me. As soon as I believed it was an angel, my thoughts of what I was seeing were answered. I rocked in severe pain and joy, while the light gave a distinct presence of a form about nine feet tall. The presence was a white-robed being with gold cuffs on His sleeves. There was a gold band around the waist of his garment. The form was a white light of radiant power. I tried to look upon his face, but I couldn't see it. My thoughts of, "Who are you?" were answered with the name Michael.

A voice from the Lord entered my mind. "Kurt, I sent this angel to protect you."

Another voice I heard was from the angel, who said, "The Lord sent me to protect you." The angel approached, and I felt it embrace me. The unbelievable energy I experienced within the arms of this majestic being brought me to joyous tears. I felt no resistance to drawing into his presence of pure white light.

A loud voice came to me: "My precious child, I will never leave nor forsake you."

The following morning, I told my mother I had to go back to Maryland. I had to return to complete the divorce and be freed from my mistake. When the divorce was settled, I called my mother, who said she had been ill. I felt I needed to see her and told her I wanted to visit. When I arrived, she was extremely ill and had to be taken to the hospital.

After a week of investigating her illness, the doctors informed me that she had only three months to live. I doubted them and believed God would decide that. I told my mother I would stay and take care of her. I felt in my heart that I had never honored my mother, and that's what my next purpose was. My mother was suffering, and I did my best to take care of her. I began reading *A Gift of Love* to her. The three months came and went. Then, three years came and went. During this time, I was becoming her son, and she was becoming my mother. She found a reason to live: she wanted to give me a nice place to live and to cook for me. We laughed over the alcoholism that had all but destroyed both our lives at one time. We talked of God's grace, which allowed us both to have another chance. One day, we were having a bitter dispute over our past behaviors. I was about to leave in anger when I finally asked, "What do you want from me?"

She said, "I need you to forgive me."

I replied, "I need you to forgive me too." We both cried and hugged. I think it was the first time we ever hugged. It felt awkward. I looked out the window at a rainbow in the sky and recalled reading about God's promise not to destroy the earth. The rainbow was a reminder of that promise.

I began to write a lot of poetry about God. I would go to bed, wanting to go to sleep, but a small voice would say, "I will not let you sleep until I am set free on paper." I would get up, write a poem or two, and then go to sleep. I completed another book of poetry.

The three years doubled to six, and I began trying to make amends with my dad, as I had with my mother. I was not that successful. I could not find forgiveness for my dad. Mom and I were doing well, and my dad and I were not. Running from pain I experienced with him once sent me to Las Vegas. I did not know I would go there; I just knew I was going for a ride one day to get away. When I got to New York, I decided to go somewhere I had never been and do what I once dreamed. I headed west, taking photographs all the way to Las Vegas.

I saw this country with a love, joy, and freedom I wish everyone could experience. I stayed in Las Vegas for two weeks. I visited the Grand Canyon and was awestruck at the majesty of God's creation. It was so amazing and beautiful. I was glad I took the trip west and fulfilled a desire of my heart.

I returned to Maine to check on my mother. She was still ill, to some degree. I stayed at her home in case she fell or needed to go to the doctor or the hospital. I stayed until I got so emotionally drained I had to take another trip. I went to Florida to visit my dad and try to reconcile. We still had extreme differences and severe emotional outbursts, which made it difficult to be around each other. I enjoyed going home to my mother's house, since I had never really had a safe place to live while I was growing up. She told me I always had a place to call home. I was glad God restored my mother to me so I could be a good son to her.

My mother and I talked a lot, and I learned exactly how much trouble I had caused her. My mother commented on how hard it was for her the night I broke my back. She had to walk to the hospital in the wee hours of the morning. When the hospital called her, they only told her I was there, and she walked with dread all the way to the hospital. She told me she used to sit up, waiting for me to return from time out drinking and smoking dope. When she heard the wind chimes on the back door, she knew I was home for the night, and she could go to sleep. Understanding these stories, I returned home with a gift for her. I placed a set of wind chimes up in the doorway and told her, "Mom, whenever you hear these wind chimes, I want you to know God brought me home safely."

Role Models

After my dad returned from Florida to Maine, I decided to take another trip. The experience of taking care of Mom was emotionally challenging. After my dad returned, I felt my relationship with him was still severely strained. His visits to the house became extremely controversial. Why he insisted on telling me how I should be living my life seemed unjustified. We still could not see eye to eye. I knew unforgiveness was my problem.

I drove down to Arkansas to meet Betty and Tim. Betty lived in the Ozark Mountains with Tim. I met Betty online in a chat room for singers and artists. I used to go online to read my poetry, and Betty went online to sing songs. Betty once asked me how I was doing, and I admitted I was stressed out. Reading poetry was a pleasant diversion from taking care of Mom. Betty invited me to come to the Ozark Mountains and take a break from the emotional strain. I needed a break from the situation between Mom, Dad, and myself, so I agreed to work for Betty in exchange for a room and food. I posted another ad for part-time work at the local post office in the town of Leslie, Arkansas. I needed some money. I felt so relaxed in the mountains I wanted to stay awhile. My ad for handyman services got me a call from a woman named Carol.

Carol owned a thousand acres of property. She needed someone to tear out the barbed wire fencing along the road to her house. Carol's six-bedroom home was three miles from the front gate. The opportunity to stay busy awhile and make a little money ensured I could stay in the mountains. It was really peaceful and nice to work outside and enjoy nature as I removed the fencing.

My ad in the post office also brought a call from a man named Jerry, who lived on top of a mountain called Peter Point. Jerry and Sally owned three hundred acres. Their house was self-sufficient: it operated under wind and solar power, though they had a generator for help. This way of living seemed amazingly wonderful to me. Jerry told me he needed the dead trees around his home taken down and cut into firewood.

Jerry, Carol, and Betty kept me busy while I stayed in the Ozark Mountains of Arkansas. God blessed me with three people who could teach me things of great value. Betty's property was two acres of overgrown brush and fallen trees. I worked to clear the land and create a yard. Betty began working with me, as the yard of her dreams began to become a reality. Betty became a good friend while I stayed with her and Tim.

One day I was working on the fence at Carol's place, and she came by. She mentioned possibly having another job for me. Carol wanted me to stop by the house before leaving that day. After work, I went to her house. I knocked on the door and walked in. Carol stood watching me and then looked at her cat a few times. Carol said, "I am not sure. Can you come see me tomorrow?" After I finished work the following day, I went back to Carol's house. I knocked on the door and she let me in. Carol looked at me and then at the cat, who was looking at me. I slouched down, and the cat ran over to me. Carol smiled and said, "Wow, you got the job. She doesn't like anybody. What I needed to know was if she likes you. I am going on a trip for a month, and you can stay here at the house and feed the cat. While I am away, you can also do some other chores I want done for extra money." Carol would go on long trips, and I would house-sit for her. I was blessed to be so trusted.

Jerry was a most fascinating gentleman. I walked into his home after cutting wood all day. The first thing I saw were eleven gold medals and one silver medal hanging on the wall; they were the kind of medals Olympians receive. I asked what the medals were for, and Jerry told me about winning the medals in the Culinary Olympics. Jerry was the captain of the American culinary team. It was incredible. I was invited to stay for dinner. There I was, sitting at the dinner table with a man who could be considered one of the best chefs in the world. I actually had tears roll down my face after tasting the food, and my body responded with a feeling of rejoice. I had never experienced such pleasure in having something to eat as I did over dinner that night.

Jerry encouraged me to continue writing. He was a wise old man and often talked about business principles. Promoting oneself seemed to be his method of achieving success. Jerry encouraged me to continue writing and to promote my book of poetry. I went to the local newspapers and told them part of my story. They published a small article about my book and me.

Among my book promotions were a few autograph parties I set up at two bookstores and a library before I told the newspaper. I met a man named John, who came to the library on the day of my autograph party. He introduced himself as the president of the Marion County Literacy Council. He was impressed with my story and the book. John invited me to a dinner theater in a nearby town. John told me it would be a nice place for me to read some of my poetry. John and I went to the dinner theater, and I listened to many local musicians before John introduced me to the owner.

Gary, the owner, wanted to hear me read onstage. I took the stage with a small audience and read five poems. I walked offstage and met Gary, who was standing and smiling. Gary handed me some money and remarked that it was not customary for performers to be paid. He said some of his patrons heard me reading and wanted to show their appreciation in the form of the money. I was overwhelmed with gratitude. Gary asked if I would return the following Saturday night and bring some books. I had ten books when I returned to the theater the following Saturday night. I waited my turn onstage and then got up and read several poems. When I was done, I informed the audience I had books for sale. I sold all ten books. Gary was thrilled and invited me to come for a special day of celebrating the work of local artists. His invitation was intimidating, as he requested if a radio station could interview me. People from the radio station would be at the dinner theater, promoting the theater and the works of local artists. I agreed, and when people heard me on the radio, they came by for an autographed book. I was truly under what I called "amazing grace."

It was a most wonderful time in my life, and I made good money working. I saved enough to plan a trip around the country. First, I would drive to Maine to see my mom and then drive west, along the top of the country, to Idaho and down the West Coast to Arizona. I would travel back east along the southern part of the country until I reached Arkansas. I purchased a tent and began my tour of the United States.

Finding Myself

I enjoyed traveling and photographing the many interesting places along my journey. I drove until I was tired and then either pitched a tent at a campground or got a hotel room. The various changes in geography were so profound and exciting to photograph. Mother Nature's mysterious forms were beautiful. God's amazing wildlife kept me in great anticipation of what was going to be revealed traveling down the road.

One day, I found a most peculiar animal along with strange cactus in the Arizona desert. The sun was blazing hot in the Arizona desert, and I was driving back to the Ozark Mountains. The speed limit was seventy-five, and I was cruising along the highway. I spotted a puppy, sitting under a guardrail alongside the highway. I pulled the car over and backed up. I wanted to be sure that what I saw was a puppy. I was surprised to find a little black and white puppy way out in the desert, with nothing around for miles. The puppy staggered out from under the guardrail toward me. He was near death, as I poured him some water. The little puppy drank almost a pint of water that I had in my car.

I put the puppy in my car and began driving again. The heat was unbearable, and there was no one to be found for miles. I looked down at the puppy, and he looked up at me as if to say, "Mister, you just saved my life." I found a small town down the road, where I could get the puppy some food. I was on a Navajo Indian reservation, getting this puppy a couple of cans of dog food at a Wal-Mart. I looked at all the Indians, wondering to whom I could give the puppy. The puppy gulped down the food and looked up at me as if to say, "Thank you. I was dying." I decided to keep the puppy as a traveling companion. I had been traveling alone on the road for almost a month. I took the dog and continued east out of Arizona and into New Mexico.

I reached the city of Albuquerque and decided to get a hotel for the night. I washed the puppy and put him in the bed beside mine. I climbed into my bed, glad that I was not tenting. I awoke to find out just how sick the puppy was. I found a mess of vomit on the bedding and two messes on the floor. I cleaned the place, hoping to reach Arkansas this day. It was another hot day, and at each rest stop, the little puppy went under the car, seeking shade and refuge from the heat.

Texas was a very long drive. I had lunch in Waco and a late dinner in Dallas. I rested another night, and the next morning, I drove into Arkansas. I was relieved to be back in the mountains.

The puppy and I visited Betty's home first. Betty was kind enough to let me keep the dog, but it had to stay outside. I grew very fond of the puppy and named him The Bandit. The Bandit was a smart-enough puppy to go away from the house to take care of business. Once I placed a piece of hot dog under his nose and said sit. I pushed The Bandit's butt down to make him sit and then gave him the hot dog. Then, I showed The Bandit a piece of hot dog and said sit, and the puppy sat. I kept the puppy close to me for a few days at Betty's before I had to go to work at another place.

I took The Bandit to a house that needed the grass cut. I was anxious to finish cutting the grass, so I could go swimming at the river after work. I let The Bandit out to run around while I cut the grass. I cut everything but what was under my car. I jumped into my car to move it. I did not see The Bandit and believed it was safe to move the car. I felt the car run over something. I remembered The Bandit liked to lie under the car. My heart sank, and I pleaded my hope I had not run over The Bandit.

I jumped out of my car and spotted the puppy on its back, his legs wiggling in the air. I ran over to find I had run over The Bandit, and his head was almost crushed. I yelled, "No," and went down on my knees, begging God to show mercy. The puppy fell limp, and I was devastated by the extreme grief in my heart. I got up, yelling at

God, wanting to know why He had given me something to love and then had taken it away. I bounced between raging mad and crying hysterically. I could not believe I killed The Bandit after saving his life.

I was grief stricken. I decided to bury him on Betty's property. I found a nice spot under a cedar tree and buried the little puppy. After the burial, I still felt so deeply hurt in my heart. I just wanted to go somewhere and sleep. I hoped when I awoke I would not be in so much pain. Sleep was the only way I could escape the grief.

I drove off into the woods to sleep in my car. I was sleeping when I began having a vision. I saw the puppy walk over to me. I reached down to pet him, and my hand passed right through his body. He was a spirit of light. The Bandit looked right at me, and I heard, "I forgive you, Kurt. I know you did not mean to do it." The Bandit in spirit walked away, and when he turned back, I heard, "I am in a much better place now."

I awoke from the vision and immediately asked, "God, what are you doing?"

I heard a voice say, "The puppy served his purpose." I then felt what seemed like a hand in the wound of my grief-stricken heart, a hand that was pulling out the pain. I asked what was going on and heard, "Kurt, do you remember those first feelings of pain when you lost something you loved?"

I felt like I was traveling back to when I was a little boy and saw my dad walking out the door. I said, "Yes."

"That's when grief was born in your heart, when your dad left."

"I was mad at you, God, for taking him away."

The loving voice said, "Yes, Kurt, your dad left you, but he never stopped loving you."

A sharper voice exclaimed to me, "Now, that beast Satan was trying to steal your affection. Do not be afraid any longer of what Satan is going to do. Remember, I sent you the Archangel Michael to take care of Satan. Michael will crush his head. You need to forgive your father, and I never left you." The pain of grief was gone. My heart was healed. Now, I understood why I could not get along with my dad. I had believed he did not love me, and that's why he left.

I was glad Carol called and that she was going on another trip. I felt saved and could go stay at her home. I lived at Carol's and worked for three weeks. Carol returned and I was paid. I left Carol's place to go see Jerry up on the mountain. Jerry was leaving to go out west and have Thanksgiving with his son. I stayed in the guesthouse that night, feeling that I was missing something. The lights went out, and I had to go put gas in the generator. I walked about fifty feet from the guesthouse in the darkness. Then, I felt a warning that something was wrong. I turned around and went back to the cabin. I got in my car and drove to the generator shed. I gassed it up, started it, and the lights came back on. The next morning, I walked over to the generator shed. I found a big pile of bear droppings right where I had stopped and turned around. I said, "Thank you, God."

I felt something was wrong—missing—in my life. I thought about Jerry going to see his son. I decided I would go see my dad for Thanksgiving, and I packed my car for a trip to Maine. I met my dad, and we shared a Thanksgiving dinner together. I decided to stay in Maine and went to live with my mom. My mom was still ill, and a couple of nurses were taking care of her. Mom was glad I had returned. I was glad she had not died. My mother was now in her seventh year past her death sentence.

One morning, I came down the steps and saw her rocking in the rocking chair. My mother was reading a prayer book and talking aloud to God. I had a vision of how amazing grace really is. My mother was rocking away in her rocking chair, praising God. I recalled our past, when I would come downstairs after a night of drinking and smoking pot to find her passed out drunk. She was lying in her own inability to make it to the bathroom. I thanked God He had not only taken the curse of alcoholism from me but from her as well. We began daily conversations, and I found out I really had a wonderful mother. The reconciliation and amends between her and I had materialized.

I told her about traveling to all the places I had been and the things I had seen. She commented how blessed I was. She said, "Many people dream of writing a book, or they dream of traveling, and you have done both. I am proud of you, son." She also said, "Life is too short to be unhappy. If you're unhappy, stop doing what makes you unhappy."

Broken Promises

I enjoyed life with Mom. I often went fishing, and I wrote a lot of stories and poems. I built a website for my photography and poetry.

I continued to try and reconcile with my dad. Intellectually, I had forgiven him, but there was still an insurmountable barrier in my heart. My dad no longer asked me to stop drinking. He began to make comments that I should quit smoking. I would always promise I was going to quit.

I struggled with the difficulties of emotional balance between a relationship with my mom and a relationship with my dad. I was experiencing the pains of growing up. Most of my life was a series of moves called geographic cures. My mom and dad struggled with each other for years to have peace between them.

I left my mother's house after she went to live in an assisted living home. I drove across the country. I was in California when I decided to go back to the beach in Maryland. I had friends there. I took a right at Sacramento and began to cross the country. I was up in the Sierra Nevada Mountains when I heard God speak plainly to me. I was praying and worrying about money. He said, "Kurt, I will give you power to make money. I love you." I cried tears of joy.

Falling for Love Again

I drove for five days to reach Ocean City, Maryland. I arrived at six o'clock in the evening and ran into two people I knew. Reggie and Paula were both friends, and I asked Reggie about work. Reggie had some painting he needed done at one of the rental properties Paula managed. Paula was willing to let me sleep there until I completed the work. I felt God was keeping His promise. I finished the painting and had enough money to rent a room. I began to work with Reggie, who was offered a contract to build a house. We began building the house, and money was flowing in. I was able to move into a nice apartment.

One day at the beach, I met a woman named Zoe, who lived in Washington DC. I asked her to lunch, and while we were having lunch together, she mentioned that she did not date men who smoked. I wanted another date, so I told her I was going to quit smoking. Zoe believed me, and we began dating. It was not long before she brought up the fact I was still smoking. I told her I was getting ready to quit. I smoked until she asked again, and I said I would quit the next week. Zoe asked again, and I promised I would quit the next day.

My attempts to stop smoking gave me severe mood swings and unbelievable physical cravings. These experiences always ended my attempts to quit, and I picked up a cigarette again and again. I got so desperate, I went to see a psychologist for help. I told the psychologist I was suicidal, and every time I picked up a cigarette, I was killing myself. The psychologist said I was the only person she knew who had come to hide his past behind a cigarette. Thinking about what she said made me angry, so I left her office and smoked. I considered what she said and believed that if I were hiding my past behind a cigarette, I was also hiding my future. I was still desperate to quit smoking and stop killing myself.

I smoked when I was not with Zoe. When I was with her, I tried to cover up the fact I was still smoking. Mouthwash, cough drops, and brushing my teeth became endless new habits. One time, Zoe asked me to do something for her. I said, "In a few minutes," and went outside to smoke.

I came in to see what Zoe wanted, and she declared that I was an addict. She was so mad. "I wanted you to do something for me five minutes ago, and smoking was more important than me."

That statement pierced my heart but was not enough to make me stop smoking. Another time, I snuck out to have a cigarette, and when I returned, Zoe asked me if I had smoked. I said no, and she called me a liar, that she could smell it, and I stunk. I was sinking deeper into hopelessness and was more desperate to quit. In her eyes, I was now a nicotine addict and a stinking liar.

I hated myself for not being able to quit smoking. I tried swearing off cigarettes, chewing gum, and wearing nicotine patches. I went to smoking cessation classes and tried medication. The medication had severe and awful side affects that only gave me excuses to be unreasonable. Even I found it almost unbearable to be around me.

One day, I was at work with Reggie. We were putting up drywall, and he asked me to nail a two by four to the wall. I had to make a brace for the walk plank. We needed one to stand on to drywall the ceiling. I did not want to go to the truck for nails, so I looked on the floor. As I picked up three nails, I thought, *That's all it took to hold Jesus to the cross.* I nailed up the plank, and Reggie and I began putting drywall on the ceiling.

The brace for the walk plank did not hold up, and we fell. I hit so hard I knocked the wind out of myself before collapsing to the floor. I lay there, unable to move. I was trying to catch my breath. My back had pain I thought would go away after I caught my breath. I thought if I could just catch my breath, I would be okay. But, I was not okay, and I left work to go home. I could barely drive home and was still trying to catch my breath.

When I arrived home, I thought a hot shower would help my back pain. I emerged from the shower and sat on the chair in my bedroom. I looked across the room at the telephone. I was in severe pain and could not get up to walk over to it. My breathing decreased to what seemed like my dying breaths. My body was in unbearable pain. I could only utter a prayer: "Lord, I know you are here. I need your help now. I cannot move and get help."

I was sitting in the chair buck naked when I heard a small voice answer, "Kurt, I once was naked and ashamed and full of pain. If someone saw you right now, would you let him help you? Would you ask for help?" I said yes and instantly I felt released from the paralyzing pain. I began to breathe and feel better. I slowly reached down to slip on my boxer shorts and cover my shame of being hopelessly naked to the world. I heard a voice again say, " Kurt, three nails did not hold me to the cross."

One day, out of the blue, my dad called. He never called me. On hearing of my accident, he invited me to come back to Maine and stay with him until I healed. I had a month to get ready to move. Most of that time, I stayed on the couch.

I did not have the rent money and wondered how I was going to pay it. I placed a pile of stuff outside the door. It was stuff I wanted to put in the dumpster the next day. Piling the stuff outside the door was all I could do, as pain told me what my limits were. As I placed the last couple things out on the porch, my neighbor came home. She asked, "What are you doing with that stuff?"

I said, "I am going to throw it away tomorrow, when I can put it in the dumpster."

She said, "Oh no, you're not. I want to buy those books!"

"Well, come on inside. I am selling everything. I hurt my back and am moving to Maine for a while." She walked through my apartment and picked out everything she wanted. She handed me six hundred dollars when she came back the next day to get her stuff. The rent was due in two days, and it was six hundred dollars. God was doing for me what I could not do for myself.

Back home with my father, my smoking interfered with his lifestyle and caused trouble between us. I went on another mission to quit smoking. I promised my father I would quit. I broke his heart when it lasted only a week. But, my attempt to quit gave me deeper insight as to why I smoked. Clearly, I saw my unresolved pain as unforgiveness. I began smoking thirty years ago to hide the shame of my childhood. I was in rebellion to cover the pain of betrayal: the betrayal of my father's promise to never leave again after walking out on my mother when I was a little boy.

My life took a severe turn for the worse when he left. I believed my father's promise and then I was sent to live with my sister faraway. My father and I made little progress toward reconciliation. There was a sticking point, and neither of us would back off from it. My father would not take responsibility for his choices that left me alone and unprotected as a little boy. Where was he when I needed protection? I would not take responsibility for how I reacted to his choices to leave. One day, a nasty argument had me deciding to head on down the road again, unable to forgive him. I just left when life was painful. This became a pattern created in my personality while growing up. I learned running away was the solution. Whenever life was a threat, I would not get what I wanted, or lose what I had, I always found a way to leave. It was my turn to leave my father in the same manner he left me. I could not admit to him exactly why I hated him for leaving.

A Whole New Life

Arkansas, Missouri, Illinois, Indiana, Ohio, Pennsylvania, New York, Massachusetts, New Hampshire, Maine, Vermont, Ohio, Michigan, Indiana, Illinois, Wisconsin, Minnesota, South Dakota, Wyoming, Montana, and Idaho. Utah, Nevada, Colorado, Kansas, Nebraska, Iowa, Florida, Georgia, Mississippi, South Carolina, North Carolina, Virginia, Maryland, Delaware, New Jersey, Kentucky, West Virginia, Tennessee, Rhode Island, New Mexico, Texas, Oklahoma, Connecticut, and California. I had been blessed to see all these states as well as Niagara Falls, the Grand Canyon, a cougar, a grizzly bear, a coyote, buffalo, the Rocky Mountains, the Blue Ridge Mountains, the Ozark Mountains, the Arizona desert, the Great Plains, Mt. Rushmore, the Black Hills, the Great Lakes, Yellowstone National Park, Old Faithful, elk, moose, and mountain sheep.

I wanted to go someplace I had not been. Louisiana was one of a few states I had not visited. I began my trip south to New Orleans, which seemed like a new and wonderful opportunity. I stopped in Maryland to visit a few people. One guy was a man named Pat. Pat asked if I wanted to spend a couple nights at his house before heading south to New Orleans. He needed some help, and for a few days, I worked for him and was very well paid. Pat offered me a permanent job, and I decided not to go to New Orleans. One week later, Hurricane Katrina leveled the city. I said, "Thank you, God, for your protection and care. You make my life so much better, because I know you're in it."

I began to build a new life from scratch, with Pat as my new employer. I worked hard and enjoyed the work I was asked to do. I visited several condos each day around the beach. It was my job to do janitorial and landscaping work and keep the places looking nice. I loved the opportunity to meet the people who came to the beach for their vacation. I found a nice place to live, and not long after that, I had a newer truck.

I became obsessed with trying to stop smoking. I could not believe I had chosen to smoke over dating Zoe. I would swear I was not going to smoke anymore, only to fail after twenty minutes. I would get so mad, I would tear up my cigarettes and toss them in the garbage. I would get down on my knees and beg God for help. I would stand, and twenty minutes later, I was fishing those torn cigarettes out of the trash. I would scotch-tape them together so I could smoke. I needed that nicotine and was seriously hooked on it. I was hopeless and helpless and at the mercy of nicotine addiction. Cigarette smoking was causing me a slow death. Somewhere I had once heard that I had a nicotine demon!

I tried church, and one particular sermon made complete sense to me. It was about the time Jesus cast out an evil spirit from someone. That spirit goes out into the desert and wanders around with no place to dwell. It then finds seven spirits worse than he is and leads them back to the man, who they enter. The man is then seven times worse off than before. I believed that to be my case.

I went to church, and the preacher prayed, asking in the name of Jesus Christ that the spirit of nicotine be cast out. One week later, I let the desire for nicotine back in, and now I was in deep trouble. I was spiritually, emotionally, mentally, and physically unable to quit smoking. I sat alone, thinking of the one thing Zoe had said that was now burning in my soul. She had once told me I was going to die alone, with my little pack of cigarettes. I began to believe it. My soul was trapped in a box, like the devil had said so long ago. I was defeated, and a pack of cigarettes ruled my life. I prayed and got a call from Jerome. He had quit smoking. He suggested I try the using the same principles Ed taught me. So, on January 14, 2007, I had my last cigarette.

Minding My Own Business

Pat became very ill with brain cancer. He wanted to let me go so he could save money for his medical bills. When a couple of the condo associations of the buildings I worked for found this out, they wanted to keep my services. I prayed and thanked God for helping me learn to mind my own business.

In learning to say prayers, I was told to be careful about what I prayed for. One night, I was walking along the boardwalk part of the beach. I noticed that the Lions Club was having a raffle for a new, red Mustang convertible. I purchased tickets for the raffle and walked away, saying a prayer. I said, "Lord, I would like to have a car like that." The next morning, I was at work cleaning the parking lot and came across an unusual car. It was a red Mustang convertible the size of a matchbox. I laughed as I picked up the little car. I recalled what I said in my prayer the night before: I had asked for a car like that.

A different experience when seeking purpose and meaning occurred while I was sitting in front of the television. I was complaining about stuff in my life I did not want and stuff that was not in my life that I wanted. I heard a small voice say to me, "Kurt, pick up that pencil, and write down what I am going to say to you." I did not pay attention.

The television picture froze; an image of a man was stuck on the screen. The sound of the television was silenced. I stared at that image in a completely quiet living room. I heard quit sharply and more loudly, "Kurt, pick up your pencil, and write down what I am going to say to you." I grabbed my pencil and sat waiting for what I might hear next. I heard these words, "Listen, I gave you the gift to be able to read, and you have read what I wanted you to read. I gave you the gift to write, and you have written what I wanted you to write. Do not attempt to add or subtract from your life. You can't. If anything needs to be added to your life, I will add it, and if anything needs to be subtracted from your life, I will subtract it. You are loved more than you can imagine. I am your God."

Abiding Love

When my dad called me to come to my stepmother's funeral, it was an invitation I could not deny. My father was broken, weeping in grief over the loss of his wife. I considered this request a total interruption of my life. My summers were devoted to my business, and it was a challenge to honor my father's request. I had to be there for my stepmother's memorial, but I did not want to go and give up my business opportunities. At the last moment, I decided to go and called both parents to tell them I would be there.

I found myself stepping out in complete faith. I trusted it was okay and left Ocean City driving to Baltimore.

I got a hotel room for the night near the airport for an early flight to Maine. I went to a nice restaurant and had a wonderful dinner. I awoke at five o'clock in the morning, went to the airport, and got a ticket to fly to Portland, Maine. I arrived in Portland at ten o'clock and went to a car rental agency. I rented a nice car and drove to Augusta. I stopped at Sears for a change of clothing. I knew I was only going for one day and I had only the clothes I was wearing when I left Maryland. I told the store clerk I needed to change and that I was going to visit my mother and my father. I purchased a new suit, shirt, shoes, tie, and belt. The cashier announced that I was rather handsome as I left the store.

I drove to see my mother at the assisted living home. My mother sat on the edge of her bed, waiting for me to visit. I entered her room, and she lit up like a light. My mother smiled as she said, "Oh my God.

You look so good, son. Wow, you look good, I am so proud of you."
I heard love speaking to me.

I said, "Mom, I have to go see Dad and be there for him." My
mother was aware of why this was so important. I visited her for a
while before leaving.

I drove over to the church where the services were to be held. I
walked into the church, unrecognized by my father. I was about seven
feet away from him before he recognized me. He looked broken. In
a sorrowful voice, he said, "My son, my son, I am so glad you're
here."

I requested to speak during the services to honor my stepmother,
who had been a small but very important influence in my life. I was
called by the pastor to come up and say a few words. I stood before
those attending the service. I looked at my dad, sitting in the front row.
He was broken-hearted, with soulless eyes. He had a dark gloomy
look on his face. I shared what was in my heart about my stepmother
and how she was a friend to us. I told of her being the "other woman"
at first and how she became my wonderful stepmother.

I left the altar to return to my seat, and I watched the miracle.
First, a gleam appeared in my father's eye. Then a light came upon
his countenance, and he smiled cheerfully. As he hugged me, he said,
"I am so proud of you, son. I love you." In my spirit, I heard that
love, freely given, surely brings a full return. It was not enough that
I forgave my father; I had to demonstrate my love to him.

The next hour we spent together after the service was filled with
both of us chatting back and forth to each other. This time was quite
unlike when he met me at the airport so long ago and the hour of
silence that followed.

During our conversation, he asked me, "Son, how much money
did you spend to get here?"

I replied, "Never mind, Dad, it was all worth it to come see
you."

"No, how much did it cost? I want to know."

I said, "About a thousand dollars, with the hotels, clothes, food,
car, and flights."

He asked me to stand and hold out my hand. I did, and he placed twenty-one hundred dollar bills in the palm of my hand. He said, "I want you to know God has been good to me too. I love you, son."

Love freely given surely brings a full return.

The best conversation I had with my father came later, during another visit to see him near Christmas. We sat at the dinner table and I explained what I had so long hidden from him. My return to reconcile with my father was much like the Bible story of the Prodigal Son. In the Bible story, the son received a ring, a robe, and sandals, and the father killed the fatted calf. When I got home with my dad, he gave me a ring, purchased me a new suit and shoes, and took me out for a steak dinner.

To my surprise, I saw that it was my doubt that God loved me that proceeded the belief that my father did not love me. I decided in my heart that I would go out of my way to understand and help my dad. The desire for a white Christmas became a reality, as a couple days before Christmas, two feet of snow fell. The second night of the snowstorm, my father, he was eighty-five, wanted some ginger ale. He told me he was going to the store. It was late at night, and I said, "No, Dad. Stay here. I will go for you." With the winds blowing snow and the roads covered in snow, I drove in the hazardous weather to the small town of Manchester to get his ginger ale. On my way, I thought of the many times I had gone out in hazardous storms to get myself a drink. Now, I was risking my life to get my father a drink of ginger ale, because I said I would help him.

The small store had no ginger ale. I decided to have a couple more near-death experiences and go to the next town. Why not? My dad wanted a drink of ginger ale. I drove in the snow to the town of Augusta, over ten miles away.

I went into a grocery store, found a twelve-pack of diet ginger ale, and brought it to the cashier. I noticed her name tag, which read Gabi. I inquired if her name was Gabrielle. She smiled and said yes. I asked, "You mean you were named after the archangel, Gabriel?"

She smiled and said yes. She smiled for a moment longer and then looked at me and said, "You know, you are the only one to ever make that connection."

I felt like I was covered by angel feathers. I walked away as tears streamed down my face and a warmth comforted me like none I had ever felt. I heard, "In all those storms and when you were in all those dark places, drinking and having near-death experiences, it was I, Gabriel, who protected you and was commanded to bring you home safely. I was given charge over you to keep you in all His ways." I had no fear in the storm, knowing the great love that was and is protecting me. I understood clearly the mystery of the spirit that had entered my heart so long ago at Christmas, when I looked out the window to see two angels made from love. For the first time in more than forty years, I spent Christmas with my mom and dad.

A Vision

Long ago, I went to a Kingdom of Light, and it was explained to me that I had a purpose. I was given what I needed to fulfill that purpose. When I met with Ed, I saw the light in his eyes and remembered the light I saw the night of my car accident. Ed spoke of unconditional love, and I was told of a kingdom, twelve by twelve, a way of life within a set of principles for living handed down by God. This design for life would bring, health, wealth, and happiness, God promised. I was handed that little book and asked to read each step for ten days. I wanted to be a free man and have a whole new life. Ed talked of the everlasting gospel of a gift of love.

One night at Ed's house, he asked me to listen to a song called, "In the Eyes of a Child." I was told to ask in the Name of the Father, the Son, and the Holy Spirit for the Lord to give me a vision. I listened to the words of this particular song as it played. I sat on the couch with my eyes closed. The song began, and I had a vision of flying above green meadows, fields, and a farm. Suddenly, there appeared an eagle in the sky, and I was heading straight toward it. I flew into the eagle's eye. Then, I was flying and seeing the same green meadows and fields as before, but I was now the eagle. I saw that same farmhouse, as I soared around over the countryside.

The song ended, and so did that vision. Ed asked me what I had seen, and I explained everything but the fact that I became the eagle. While still amazed at having such a vision, he asked, "Why did you not tell me you were the eagle?" I couldn't believe he knew! He was telling me about the gifts of God: choice, voice, vision, feeling, and manifestation.

It was over five years later before I was reminded of that vision in a most unusual way. I was watching a video of a gospel singer Vern Jackson on the television network TBN. In his video, I saw the same countryside, farmhouse, and eagle that had been in my vision. I learned the video was made in Israel.

I found the darkness of my past was hiding behind my disbelief in God. As I increasingly believed and followed the spiritual path of unconditional love, my life was transformed into the light of a beautiful future. The path I followed meant taking steps necessary to give up the darkness and walk in the light. Unforgiveness was my last stronghold. I had deep pain and was broken and missing until I returned to God. I finally got what Ed had said about my car crash: I did not have to die, and someone already had

I have been in the mercy seat of God. I came to believe in Jesus Christ. He is the Lord and Savior of my life. My life was about absolution and atonement. When Ed gave me the ten-day plan of reading each principle in the little book, he promised me that after ninety days, I would inherit all of Gods promises in Psalms 91 (Thompsons Chain Reference Study Bible) NIV.

It was not my intent to grow up and become a drunken, drug-addicted, illiterate criminal who never had a chance of having a dream. Writing this book was one of my dreams. But for the grace of God, I do not feel alone or separated any longer. I feel loved and comforted and assured that my own life's destiny will remain secure as long as I try to find and do the will of My Creator. It was through my searching that I was often confronted with the supernatural. It was easy to get confused between the real and unreal as I learned more about an all-powerful, all-knowing, and loving Creator, who was to become my friend. Only a friend would say and do this for me.

In my attempt to bring this story to an end, I am left with this last concept to consider. Reading the Bible, as I have in my journey, left me with one last, strong consideration of my purpose here on earth. I have read the Bible cover to cover twice, Genesis to Revelation. On completing it, my second desire was to fill my mind with its contents. I closed the cover and asked God, "What is this book all about?"

A still, small voice answered, "It's all about you and me!"

B.I.B.L.E.
Basic Instructions Before Leaving Earth

I hope you will seriously consider where you will end up when your life ends. Thank you for reading this book.

Angel Love

In the silent serenity of night's darkest hour,
the light of a full moon glows
revealing Heaven's power.
Soft moonbeams of satin flowing down behind a cloud,
angels dance and others sing loud.
I often wonder why I see them this way,
tears come to flowing
and I wish everyone could see them, I say.

It is a gift of mine to see them in the light,
a vision to behold and one to write.
For in the silent serenity of night's darkest hour
is when Heaven flows with its mighty power.
Bringing us gifts to wherever we are,
making our lives shine bright as a star.

Before you get old,
you ought to be told.
A great light shining from above
a reflection that we are truly made of love.
On any other day, in every other way,
all I will ever really want to say.
This that I do is because ...
I too ... Love you.

A New Love

I believe love is a perfect gift with its own fate.
It always arrives on time, never late.
Each day that is passing is love's date.
Everyone has love as a helpmate.

Love is coming, begin to shout.
Love is coming, there is no doubt.
Love is coming to bring us out.
Love is all, life is about.

My dream is to find a love for me only.
I see it in the mirror that reflects me as lonely.
What mends the heart that is breaking?
When love is only in the making.

Love is coming, begin to shout.
Love is coming, there is no doubt.
Love is coming to take us out.
Love is all, life is about.

Just what do you do
To keep love from walking out on you?
Left not knowing when,
it will return again.
Love alone is a precious gift of surprise.
Precious it is, to look in the mirror
as love twinkles in my eyes.

Share the gift of love with one you do not know.
Care about the one you love before you go.
Do it now, before the passing of years.
Do it now, before the falling of tears.

A Plan

Please, Lord God, help me follow your plan.
Grant me the faith that says I can.
Help me, Holy Spirit, to become able,

Lord Jesus the Christ, we say,
Thank you, for the offer to share your cup.
I was thirsty and you said: Come and drink up.
I was so dirty and cried, as you washed me,
I was so blind to see.
I ran to and fro, like a little mole,
searching for safety, in the right hole.
You cleaned the wounds and scars of my soul.

Yes, I was running away and lost.
'Til the day you said: There is no cost.
You told, from stories of old.
That it was free and you had come for me.
I then began to see,
the Shadow of The Almighty had fallen on me.

Like a beacon of light, from a high tower,
you called me out, it was my hour.
You called me your friend and said I was yours,
It was so beautiful that you opened the doors.

Remember you said, at the last hour.
You have been given the power.
The Love that you need
it is with the children of the light—my seed.

A Prayer

Dear Lord Jesus Christ,
please hear my words to say.
We give you praise, honor, and glory today.
Let us come together under your Holy Name,
each time we do we are never the same.
Help us rejoice, to why you came.
For you alone, are The Most High One,
we give thanks to God for His begotten Son.
The only God there is above,
to free us by the blood of His great love.

Dear Lord Jesus the Christ,
please hear what I say,
this is my prayer for today.
Thank you for the breath of life

I am willing to love you, more than anything.

What was I doing when you came to call.
Yes, I was sleeping when you asked for my all.
I was totally lost,
searching for the cost.
Just a little sip of hope,
I no longer wanted to use the dope.

Who was that man to come around?
Do you know where I was found?
On the ground,
asking for help, with a please.
I could not get up off my feeble knees.
I just did not know,
to the cross I would go.

Come Here! Come Here!
Bring your life to me,
so blind to the cross, I still could not see.
Go away I cried, without a care why you died.
I was going to hell's party
because you I denied.
What my life said was a sad report,
anything for your glory I fell short.

From within the bondages of pain
came a release.
Under the wings of His Spirit,
a whisper to my ear.
Listen you may hear.
My precious child, I give you my peace.
Remember I am here.
With a touch of His grace,
hope glowed on my face.
It was only by your great love,
for faith to stay in the race.

So awesome your mercy,
given when I did not deserve,
I hope that others understand
the Living Christ I serve.
Many have spoken that I am crazy,
for want of things of the world, I became lazy.
They say stay away.
He is very odd.
For when I love to speak,
it is about the love of God.

Show me the way, Lord, as my spirit sings,
teach me about all things.
How to better give praise, honor, and glory
to the King of Kings.

Lord Jesus Christ,
please hear my prayer today.
This is all that I can say.
I am willing to love you, more than anything.
Thank you for the breath of life

God, I thank you for humbling me,
the glory of your Son is Majesty.

I am glad for the little I understand
and to see the power of your hand.

Truly, Lord, my heart you have won.
Thank you, Lord, Thy Will Be Done.

Thank you, Lord, for giving me a look.

It was such an awesome story,
about The Living God and His glory.

A precious gift to set us free,
from the terrible captivity.

Please, Lord, if you will
show me the way to go.
Help me tell the others that want to know.

About the hope to shine in my eyes,
that Jesus Christ will answer their cries.

A Voice and a Vision

One day, was I to lie, upon my bed.
A Voice and a Vision came into my head.
This vision of an Angel did appear to me.
The voice of this angel said:

This is to be!
Bless you as a Son.
Unconditional Love, has won!
The One that commands did hear your call.
Be ye fearless you will not fall!
When the little boy did call upon my name.
Lord of Lords and King of Kings,
I AM and came.
This gift in your life,
will be a joy for your life.
Remember the steps to deliver you from hell,
come through the gates and drink from this well.
This water of life will always flow free,
from the Thrown of The Living God
He is you SEE!!

Remember the commandments and this day!
A Light you are, to show others … The Way.

Hello!

Hello! Hello!
What do you know?
It is a privilege for me to talk.
Before I was allowed to speak,
I had to learn to walk.
I was too weak,
I was very odd, and knew nothing of God.

Told He was mad,
that was real to what I had.
Told I was bad,
and nothing I could do was better than sad.
I kept a promise to do better tomorrow,
and I lived in constant sorrow.

Then one day,
I heard someone say
there is another way.
The world said: that idea is gay.
I just stood there crying,
inside I was dying.
told to keep trying.

Then one day,
I heard someone say
there is another way.
Why don't you pray?

The world said: that idea is queer,
I was living in fear,
and had no clue, to why I was here.
All I had ever done was drink beer.

It was a painful circumstance,
I begged and pleaded for a second chance.

Then one day,
I heard someone say
there is another way.
Just pray
and ask God to help with a please.

The world said:
God does not want you.
I thought that was true.
I just lay on my sick bed,
fear ruled in my head.
I wished I was dead.

Then there came a voice from behind,
it sounded soft and kind.
I could not hear it in my mind.
I heard it in my heart.
Do you want a new start?
Are you ready for a new life?
Will you let me take your strife?

I did not know what to do,
I could not even guess.
I said: Yes!
I fell down on my knees,
and yelled to God: Help me please.

I was picked up on my feet,
what I felt was another treat.

This was a time I will not forget,
the world lost its bet.
To keep me down in a hole,
coloring my soul,

in crimson red.
With ruling fear in my head.
Telling me a lie,
you had better die
and would be better off dead.

I no longer have to hide
or think suicide.

I was granted a ride, from the valley of death.
Out before my last breath.

Lord God, thank you for removing my remorse,
I did not know you ride the white horse.

Lord God, thank you for washing away my guilt,
and leading me away
From the prison Satan built.

Lord God, thank you for the touch of your hand
and leading me into a better land.
A place I can see,
A place to be free.
A place to walk and talk with Thee.

A place to just be,
with the love between you and me.

The Light and the Way

Can you shout the "Good News" louder than me?

Can you run the good race faster than me?
After getting your back broke because you could not see.

Oh, the trouble that comes for those with no ear!
Like the darkness that swallowed me
from inside the beer.

Just stop for this moment, take a look and listen.
For the calling of God is not worth missing.

This can be the end of your walk alone through life,
and even a miracle for your friend called a wife.

For God is God and no other to be.

A beautiful Holy Spirit
Make a choice for the new life
of His eternity without end.

Come Here! Come Here!
The words to your ear,
and within the truth may you hear.
I am always near.

Then you may shout louder than me,
and begin with eyes that see.
That greater is He in me.

A precious whisper of His Promise
that this is what to do.

Call upon my name for I will not leave nor forsake you.

You were lost in the wilderness,
listening to someone who cries.

I gave you a "Spirit of The Truth" no lies.
He shall lead you in understanding not alibis.

Just think when you saw that beautiful dove,
and asked to return to your first love.

I AM Him that sits most high above.
The Light of the world listen … to my love.

For I know the numbers of your hairs,
and they will not get harmed.
I am within all your affairs,
do not get alarmed.

With any two or more it is the same,
I am standing at the door of "The Way"
That is under my name.

Who Is The One?

Who is it that stands behind me?
Who is it that I cannot see?
Each time I sit down to write?
Each time I seek The Father of Light!

Always in a soft voice:
you can do better than that.
Like an angel of mercy to sit on my shoulder,
use your faith and become bolder.

Between a dogwood on a mountain
and His right hand.
See the beautiful fountain
flowing over the promise land.

Whom you seek stands at the peak,
waiting for the weak.
Listen for His command:
Come one, come all!
Do you hear the call?
To come out from under the shame,
Jesus the Christ is His Holy Name.

Who is it that walks before me?
Who is it that talks with me?
Who is it that I cannot see?

Each time I get upset.
Each time I forget.
Each time I get uptight.
Each time I want to fight.
Each time I want to do what is right.

Always in a soft voice:
Come and sit down, here on the ground,
rest little one of mine, you have been found.

Who gives me more love than my mother?
Who gives me more love than my brother?
Who loves me more than any other?
That I have known?
Where is this place I am shown?

You have come to the end of man-made teaching,
it is your heart that I have been reaching.
A whole new start with another friend,
your broken heart will mend.

To leave your mother,
and your brother,
as well as any other that wanted you to stay,
Another day.
There is nothing wrong, lean on me and be strong.
I Am the Way you must follow.
I Am the Truth that set you free.
I Am the Life you seek to see.
Pick up your cross and follow me.

A Vision to BEHOLD

I lay upon my bed,
A vision came into my head.
I closed my eyes
and darkness filled the skies.
I saw a LIGHT coming down from above,
the Light of an Angel that appeared as a Dove.

AS THIS LIGHT SPREAD ITS WINGS,
OTHER ANGELS APPEARED WITH A GLORY THAT SINGS.

The Angel came down with darkness under His feet,
others followed and the Glory was so sweet.
When this Angel stood upon the land,
everything changed and a new vision was at hand.

Standing before me was a Mighty White Horse,
the One sitting upon him was … The Lord, of course.

A Mighty King dressed in a radiant
the others that landed behind him were also of this LIGHT.

BEHOLD was the word that came with such MIGHT.
I watched carefully as The Horse stood near,
what I was watching became very clear
His hair was like the purest of white silk,
His beard also flowed just like white milk.
The KING appeared mature but not very old,
upon His head were many crowns in one made of pure GOLD.
The others that followed were an army I was told.
Again the one Voice of many voices said … BEHOLD
I asked about his hair,
and mercy was what I saw there.
I was quite sure of what I heard,
I asked about His beard and Wisdom was the word.

It guarded His mouth as He continued to Ride.
I wanted to wait till He came to my side.
I looked up at The Powerful KING,
light flowed around me and began to sing.
A Multitude of music and all the sounds of many instruments
and singers made just one word
Victory was the only thing I heard.
Precious gems were also laden in His crown.
The KING came upon me with eyes I did see,
lightning flashed as He glanced at me.
His face shone a radiance of compassion so bold.
again The Voices of many said ... BEHOLD.
A whisper was given to my ear.
GET ON YOUR HORSE is what I did hear.
I said MY LORD ... I am but dust and mud,
His venture dripped on me and I was covered in His blood.
I saw a name written and then the Voice from above,
The Voice sang of VICTORY in The Name of Unconditional LOVE.